How to use *explore*

Issue 105

The 91 daily readings in this issue of Explore are designed to help you understand and apply the Bible as you read it each day.

It's serious!

We suggest that you allow 15 minutes each day to work through the Bible passage with the notes. It should be a meal, not a snack! Readings from other parts of the Bible can throw valuable light on the study passage. These cross-references can be skipped if you are already feeling full up, but will expand your grasp of the Bible. Explore uses the NIV2011 Bible translation, but you can also use it with the NIV1984 or ESV translations.

Sometimes a prayer box will encourage you to stop and pray through the lessons—but it is always important to allow time to pray for God's Spirit to bring his word to life, and to shape the way we think and live through it.

We're serious!

All of us who work on Explore share a passion for getting the Bible into people's lives. We fiercely hold to the Bible as God's word—to honour and follow, not to explain away.

1 Find a time you can read the Bible each day

2 Find a place where you can be quiet and think

3 Ask God to help you understand

4 Carefully read through the Bible passage for today

5 Study the verses with *Explore*, taking time to think

6 Pray about what you have read

thegoodbook COMPANY

BIBLICAL | RELEVANT | ACCESSIBLE

Welcome to *explore*

Being a Christian isn't a skill you learn, nor is it a lifestyle choice. It's about having a real relationship with the living God through his Son, Jesus Christ. The Bible tells us that this relationship is like a marriage.

It's important to start with this, because it is easy to view the practice of daily Bible reading as a Christian duty, or a hard discipline that is just one more thing to get done in our busy lives.

But the Bible is God speaking to us: opening his mind to us on how he thinks, what he wants for us and what his plans are for the world. And most importantly, it tells us what he has done for us in sending his Son, Jesus Christ, into the world. It's the way that the Spirit shows Jesus to us, and changes us as we behold his glory.

Here are a few suggestions for making your time with God more of a joy than a burden:

- *Time:* Find a time when you will not be disturbed. Many people have found that the morning is the best time as it sets you up for the day. But whatever works for you is right for you.

- *Place:* Jesus says that we are not to make a great show of our religion *(see Matthew 6:5-6)*, but rather, to pray with the door to our room shut. Some people plan to get to work a few minutes earlier and get their Bible out in an office or some other quiet corner.

- *Prayer:* Although *Explore* helps with specific prayer ideas from the passage, do try to develop your own lists to pray through. Use the flap inside the back cover to help with this. And allow what you read in the Scriptures to shape what you pray for yourself, the world and others.

- *Feast:* You can use the "Bible in a year" line at the bottom of each page to help guide you through the entire Scriptures throughout 2024. This year, the passages each day are linked, showing how God makes and keeps his promises. We're grateful to Katherine Fedor of treasureinthebible.com for her permission to use this Bible-reading plan. You'll find passages to read six days a week—Sunday is a "day off", or a day to catch up!

- *Share:* As the saying goes, *expression deepens impression*. So try to cultivate the habit of sharing with others what you have learned. Why not join our Facebook group to share your encouragements, questions and prayer requests? Search for *Explore: For your daily walk with God.*

And enjoy it! As you read God's word and God's Spirit works in your mind and your heart, you are going to see Jesus, and appreciate more of his love for you and his promises to you. That's amazing!

Carl Laferton is the Editorial Director of The Good Book Company

Spiritually healthy?

How are you doing in your Christian life? Really thriving, barely surviving, or somewhere in between? How can you even know how you're doing?

Welcome to your spiritual healthcheck as you start the new year. Over the next 16 studies, we'll move through some diagnosis questions, then identify some spiritual vitamins that will help improve your Christian health, and finish by thinking about the doctor who helps us answer the questions and enables us to self-administer the vitamins.

But first, before we get to diagnosis, we need to ask: what actually *is* a spiritually healthy Christian?

Read Romans 8:28-31

- ❷ *Who does God work for the good of (v 28—they are described in two ways)?*
- ❷ *What has God decided (predestined) he will do for those people (beginning of v 29)?*
- ❷ *Why can we be confident that this will happen (v 31)?*

When I was four, I decided to be a firefighter. When I was seven, I wanted to become a footballer. When I was nine, I was aiming to be a librarian. I failed in all three aspirations. When I was 19, God called me to faith in his Son, and I came to love him—and God decided that I would become like his Son, Jesus. And I may have changed my mind since I was four, seven and nine—but God will not change his mind, nor falter in his determination, nor fail in his ability, to turn me into someone who is just like Jesus, the perfect person.

So to be perfectly spiritually healthy is to be just like Christ Jesus. And to be growing more spiritually healthy is to be growing more like Christ Jesus.

Think about what Jesus was like during his time on earth. Kind. Compassionate. Courageous. Brave. Loyal. Wise. Thoughtful.

- ❷ *How do you feel about being like that?*

Read 1 John 3:1-2

- ❷ *When will we be completely conformed to the image of Christ (v 2)?*

Spiritual health is being just like Christ—and, until Christ returns, you won't be in full spiritual health. Sin-sickness will cling until the day he comes. But God is working for your good—for your Christ-likeness—in all things: the ups and the downs, the thrilling parts and the mundane parts, of normal life. None of us are completely Christ-like—but God is at work to make us more Christ-like. He is not content simply to save us *through* Christ; he has decided to make us *like* Christ.

⌃ Pray

Adapted from John Newton

Lord, I know I am not who I one day will be, but I thank you that I am not who I used to be. Please make me more like Christ today than I was yesterday—and please answer that prayer each day until the day I stand before him. *Amen.*

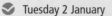

Diagnosis #1: Love?

We're going to ask five questions over five studies that help us to diagnose the state of our spiritual health, and begin to improve it. The first is: are you in love with Jesus?

You might find it very helpful to ask a Christian who knows you well this question, and the next four. Their diagnosis of you may be as accurate, or more accurate, as yours!

Good and not-so-good

Read Revelation 2:1-3

> ❓ *In what ways is the Ephesian church doing well, according to Jesus (speaking through his apostle, John)?*

> ❓ *If you had been a visitor to this church, what would you have made of it?*

Read Revelation 2:4-7

> ❓ *What is the problem (v 4)?*

The NIV84 translates verse 4 more evocatively: "You have forsaken your first love". For all that the Ephesian church are doing, serving and withstanding, there is one thing they are not doing: they are not loving Jesus.

> ❓ *How serious is this (v 5)?*

> ❓ *What does Jesus promise them if they listen, change and fall in love with him all over again (v 7)?*

How easy it is for churches, and Christians, to grow cold in our love for Jesus. At first, it seems so obvious and natural—we are awed and moved by our Saviour's love for us, and we respond by loving him. Then come the routines and the rotas, and without noticing, we end up doing the right things, but no longer really doing the one thing that matters—loving the one who has saved us. And if I am struggling in the Christian life, it is likely to be rooted in a dwindling of my love for Christ.

☑ Apply

> ❓ *Do you love Jesus? Not in a sentimental, butterfly-flapping kind of way, but in a wowed, awed, moved way?*

> ❓ *Do you love him more than you used to, or less than you used to?*

How to come back

How can you come back to, or grow in, your love for Jesus? By seeing how he loves you. Our love is kindled as we glimpse his blazing love for us. And this is great news, because we will never touch the depths or grasp the heights of his love! If you feel loveless towards Jesus, don't focus on your love for him—delight in his love for you.

Read 1 Corinthians 13:4-7

Our love for Jesus is not like this—but his love for us is always like this. Re-read these verses, replacing "Love" and "it" with "Jesus". This is how the Lord treats you. This is how he loves you—with all your flaws and failings. Don't you love him?

⬆ Pray

Read Ephesians 3:16-19 and pray for yourself what Paul prayed for his friends.

Diagnosis #2: Grateful?

Here is the second diagnosis question to help you discern your true spiritual health: are you grateful for the cross?

Notice the question is not, *do you understand the cross?* Or even, *do you tell others about the cross?* but, *are you grateful?*

To be truly grateful for what Jesus did at Calvary, we need to begin to appreciate two truths: the truth about who we are, and the truth about what he did.

Read 1 Timothy 1:15

❓ *What does Paul think of himself?*

❓ *What does Paul know about why Jesus came?*

We will not appreciate the cross until we first identify with Paul, thinking, *But in truth I am the worst of all sinners.* Think of your thoughts of anger, lust, selfishness and pride. Think of the things you have done that you are so relieved your nearest and dearest do not know about. These sins are not unfortunate slip ups, committed by a basically decent person who is generally deserving of praise. They are signs of who you are—a sinner, deserving judgment.

If this makes you feel wretched, then that is a sign that the Spirit is at work in you, since one of his works is to convict us of sin (John 16:8-11). Paradoxically, wretchedness is a sign of health—because it is only the wretched who can marvel at the cross (Romans 7:24-25); it is only the broken and humble who will be justified and exalted (Luke 18:14). If you think God accepts and loves you on the basis of anything you do—

Bible-reading, church serving, evangelising, *anything*—then you will never be able truly to appreciate the wonder of the cross.

Read Mark 15:1-39 and Isaiah 53:4-9

Reflect on all that Jesus went through on Good Friday, and as you do, repeat to yourself:

"He did that in my place, for my sake. It should have been me rejected. It should have been me punished. It should have been me forsaken. It should have been me mocked. It should have been me dying.

"But it was him. In my place, for my sake."

John Newton, the slave trader turned pastor who famously wrote the lines, "Amazing grace! How sweet the sound that saved a wretch like me", said towards the end of his life, "Although my memory is fading, I remember two things very clearly: I am a great sinner and Christ is a great Saviour". He was physically fading, but spiritually healthy.

⌃ Pray

Re-read Isaiah 53:4-9 and pause regularly to pour out your gratitude, as a great sinner saved by a great Saviour.

⌄ Apply

❓ *How will you make sure that you take time each day to admit your sin, reflect on the cross, and grow in gratitude?*

Diagnosis #3: Excited?

Here's the next diagnosis question: are you excited about the new creation? If we are not looking forward to our next life, we will never live well in this one.

Read Romans 8:18-25

The future

❷ *What does life appear to be like for Paul's first readers (v 18)?*

❷ *How does he encourage them (v 18)?*

❷ *How does creation feel about the day Jesus returns and God's children are "revealed"—that is, their status is made utterly obvious (v 19)? Why (v 20-22)?*

It is not only believers who are waiting to be made perfect—it is the world too. Creation fell when we did, it decays as we do, and it will be restored when we are.

One reason we fail to be excited about eternity is because we've bought into cultural views of "heaven"—sitting around on a cloud in a white sheet strumming a harp is no one's idea of fulfilment. The Bible shows us something very different—an eternity spent enjoying a perfect creation, in perfect bodies, in perfect relationship with others and with God—a forever of "freedom and glory" as children of God (v 21).

The feeling

❷ *How should we feel about the prospect of coming home to God as his sons (v 23)?*

❷ *How else should we wait for that (v 25)?*

We are not to settle for the best this world offers, nor despair at the worst this world inflicts. Like a fiancée waiting for her wedding day, we wait with huge excitement; but we do wait. When we fail to remember where we are headed, we grow unexcited about our future home and half-hearted in our present obedience. We feel dissatisfied so we give in to sin, because we have forgotten that real satisfaction lies ahead of us. We feel trapped by life so we seek freedom in immorality, because we have forgotten that real freedom lies ahead of us. We experience suffering so we give in to bitterness, because we have forgotten that real glory lies ahead of us.

⌄ Apply

How can you know you are eager about the new creation? Because your life would not make sense if there were no new creation. The "present sufferings" of Paul's readers only made sense if there was to be a "glory that will be revealed" (v 18).

❷ *Think about your life. Do you make decisions that only make sense because the new creation is ahead of you?*

❷ *Think about your neighbours. Do they see or hear anything different in your lifestyle and conversation that shows that you know where you are heading?*

⌃ Pray

Ask God for greater clarity about eternity and confidence that it is *your* eternity, so that you grow more excited about eternity.

Diagnosis #4: Committed?

We're now (you're probably relieved to know!) over halfway through the diagnosis of your spiritual health. Today: are you committed to God's people?

Remaining in Christ

Read John 15:9-11, 14-15

- ❷ *How do we "remain in" Jesus' love (v 9-10)?*
- ❷ *Whose joy is "complete" if we remain in Jesus' love (v 11)?*
- ❷ *How does Jesus view those who "do what I command" (v 14-15)?*

So, if you are someone who wants to grow in love for Jesus, who wants to know complete joy, who wants to be considered a friend by Jesus, who enjoys learning all that Jesus learned from his Father—then all you need to do is to "do what I command", says Jesus. And there's only one command...

The one command

Read John 15:12-13

- ❷ *What is the command (v 12)? How do we know what this involves (v 12-13)?*

Read Romans 12:9-16

Paul is giving the church in Rome some ways to demonstrate a love for God's people that is "sincere"—Christ-like. Here is how Christian love looks on any day when we are not called to die for our brothers or sisters.

- ❷ *What would each of these look like if lived out in your church?*
- ❷ *Are there any here that particularly surprise you, or challenge you?*

It is strikingly simple, and deeply challenging: our love for other believers is a Christ-given diagnostic tool for knowing if we truly love him, and are truly enjoying knowing him. It is a love that prompts and is seen in actions—honouring others, sharing with others, being hospitable to others, rejoicing and mourning alongside others.

If you do not sincerely, sacrificially, actively love God's people, then you are struggling spiritually. If you do, then you are growing spiritually. It is as simple as that.

Read 1 John 4:9-11

If you struggle to love the other members of your church, do not look inside yourself and seek to summon up feelings of love and the will to act in love. No—look outside yourself and gaze at God's act of love in sending his Son to die for you. As you look at the cross, you will love Christ; and as you look at the cross, you will see how to love his people. After all, our King says that, "Whatever you did for one of the least of these brothers and sisters of mine, you did for me" (Matthew 25:40). You love him by loving his family. He loves it when you love his family.

Apply

- ❷ *Look back at Romans 12:9-16. How are you going to love Jesus' people this week?*
- ❷ *How are you going to use the cross to motivate your love?*

Diagnosis #5: Godly?

Here, before we move on to the "vitamins", is the fifth and final question to help you assess your own spiritual health: are you pursuing godliness?

Power

Read 2 Peter 1:1-3

Peter is writing to people who have "grace and peace", with "a faith as precious as ours" (v 1-2). He is writing to Christians.

> ❷ *What does God use his power to give us (v 3)?*

"Godly" is an often-used, little-thought-about word. Godly means God-like—to live and think and feel in a situation just as God would. And we know what God would do and think and feel because of our "knowledge of him who called us". We know God's glory—literally his weight, his god-ness. We know his goodness—his love and grace.

So can you live a godly, holy life? Can you defeat that sin that keeps coming back? Can you love the Christian who hurt you greatly? Yes—by his power. You can pursue godliness. But why would you want to?

Promises

Read 2 Peter 1:4-8

> ❷ *What else has God given us (v 4)?*
>
> ❷ *What do we know we will do "through them" i.e. what has God promised (v 4)?*

One day, we will participate in the divine nature. We will not just be with God; we will be like God. We will be the people we were designed to be—in God's image; Genesis-1 people (enjoying being like God) rather than Genesis-3 people (grasping at being God).

> ❷ *What will we do if we grasp this (v 5-7)?*
>
> ❷ *What difference would it make to your life, and the lives of those around you, if you had each of these?*

Don't miss the connection between v 4 and v 5-7. Peter is saying, *Because you will one day be like God (v 4), on this day make an effort to become more like God (v 5-7)*. After all, it is Jesus—God on earth—who showcases all the qualities of v 5-7 perfectly. And as we look at Jesus' self-control, perseverance, love, etc. we see the person we'd love to be. When we see it like that, we realise that godliness is a joyful privilege more than it is a duty.

✔ Apply

> ❷ *How hard have you been pursuing godliness? How do Peter's words here motivate you to pursue it?*

God's power for you means you have no reason to fail at being godly, and no excuse for failing either.

> ❷ *How does this most challenge you?*
>
> ❷ *Think back to all five diagnostic questions. How are you encouraged? How are you humbled?*

Remember, you are saved by Christ, not by your Christian life. You may need to change; but if you are trusting in Christ, then v 3-4 are true of *you*.

Bible in a year: Isaiah 54 • Ezekiel 14 • Matthew 24 • 2 Peter 2

The route to blessing #1

We're going to spend a few Sundays understanding and meditating on Psalm 1. It tackles the fundamental question: how can I be happy?

Read Psalm 1

Focus on verse 1.

- ❓ *What is the first step towards being blessed by God?*
- ❓ *Why is this negative message so unpopular with our world today?*

The message is "repent". Being blessed by God involves turning away from practices and attitudes that may be normal, enjoyable, and even seem "sensible" to us.

Beware walking with the "wicked"

- ❓ *What do you think it means to "walk in step with the wicked"?*

It is a mistake to think that "wicked counsel" (NIV84) is limited to those who might encourage us to lie, steal or harm others. In the Bible, wickedness refers to any way of living that leaves God out of the picture. Wicked counsel is both the encouragement of friends to waste money on frivolities, and the "sensible" advice of a kindly gran who tells you to "look after number one".

- ❓ *Can you think of some subtle (and so more dangerous) ways in which people might live by "wicked" counsel?*

Care in company

- ❓ *Why is the company we keep so important?*

As any parent knows, the company we keep—the friends we choose to spend time with—is one of the most significant factors in how our character develops. Their attitudes and values can rub off on us without us noticing. And so all too easily we can find ourselves adopting the life, or "way", of "sinners"—those who deny and defy God's rule in life.

Steer clear of mockery

- ❓ *Why can mocking others be so tempting to do or to watch?*

Mockery puts us in the position of feeling we are superior to others. That makes it soul acid that eats away at us, leaving us with a distorted view of ourselves and a sneering cynicism about others.

▽ Apply

Think about your values—how you think life should be lived. Think about the friends you spend time with, the comedy shows you watch, the books you read.

- ❓ *What effect do they have on you? Could they be leading you away from enjoying life under God's rule?*
- ❓ *Are there any practical steps you need to take?*
- ❓ *Is there anything you're trying to avoid confronting? Remember—without repentance, there is no blessed life!*

Take your vitamins

Diagnosing problems can help us start to address them—hopefully you've experienced this during the last few days. And the Lord has also given us spiritual "health vitamins".

It's to these we now turn...

Bible: bad for you?

We're joining an argument between Jesus and the Jewish religious leaders.

Read John 5:39-40

- ❷ *Is the problem of these leaders that they don't read the Scriptures?*
- ❷ *So what is their problem? What are they missing?*

In Luke 24:32, two disciples describe the feeling of having a Bible study with Jesus: "Were not our hearts burning within us while he talked with us on the road and opened the Scriptures to us?" Is that regularly, or ever, your experience when you sit down to read the Bible?

The crucial detail here was not that the Scriptures were opened, but that Jesus was there. It is very easy to read the Bible intellectually—for more understanding; or morally—to live better; or mechanically—because studies like this told us it would help our faith. None of those are wrong—but on their own, they are bad for you (as they were for those religious leaders). Supremely, we need to read the Bible relationally—to meet with Jesus. Read the Bible to meet with Jesus: speak with Jesus as you read it, praise Jesus as you understand it, love Jesus more as you see his love for you—and your faith will grow stronger and your Christian life will grow healthier.

✅ Apply

- ❷ *How would you describe your approach to reading the Bible? Mainly intellectual, or moral, or mechanical, or relational?*
- ❷ *How does this affect your faith?*

🔼 Pray

Lord Jesus, you meet with me in your word. As I read it, by the work of your Spirit, please enable me not only to understand more about you but to know you better and love you more. Please make my Bible-reading relational. Amen.

Bible: at work in you

Vitamins work not only as we take them but through the day. So must God's word.

Read Psalm 119:9-16

- ❷ *What words does the writer use to describe what he does with God's word?*

Here is one way to enjoy Christ all day: set alarms for three points in the day. Read the Bible in the morning and contemplate one truth about Jesus. When the alarm goes, remember the truth, and praise him. Your enjoyment of Jesus through his word does not need to end when you close your Bible!

- ❷ *How are you proactively going to meditate upon Christ's ways each day?*

Bible in a year: Genesis 10 – 13

Learning to pray

Here's the second vitamin: prayer. If you struggle with prayer—if you need Jesus to "teach" you how to pray—you're in good company: so did Jesus' disciples.

What we say

Read Luke 11:1-4

- ❓ *Whose interests are the focus of the first half of this prayer (v 2)?*
- ❓ *Whose interests are the focus of the second half (v 3-4)?*
- ❓ *How might this order shape the way we feel, and our view of our own problems, as we pray?*

Given that Jesus also prayed using other words (e.g. Luke 10:21), and given that he habitually spent hours in prayer (e.g. Mark 1:35), it's unlikely he wanted us to see this as exact wording to say, but rather as a series of headings or topic areas.

⌃ Pray

This week, why not structure your prayers around each clause of Luke 11:2-4, taking one a day?

- Enjoy the truth it contains.
- Pray through the request.
- Ask for eyes to see the answers.

Why not start right now?!

What we most need

Read Luke 11:5-13

- ❓ *What does the person in Jesus' parable want, and why (v 5-6)?*
- ❓ *Why does he receive it (v 7-8)?*

- ❓ *What comparison does he make between flawed ("evil") human fathers and our perfect Father in heaven (v 11-13)?*

What a wonderful promise v 10 is! We should pray with confidence. And what a wonderful invitation v 8 is! We should pray with persistence. What a wonderful truth v 13 is! We should pray with assurance. It's an intriguing end to the lesson—"your Father in heaven [will] give the Holy Spirit to those who ask him!" (v 13). Notice that, in prayer, we need to learn what to ask for as much as we need to learn that God is willing, and able, to answer. In the parable, the requester was making a good request for a good reason. We are to learn to ask confidently and persistently for what we most need—and supremely, what we most need is the Spirit.

This is the wonder of prayer when it matches God's priorities—God answers by giving us new experiences of the peace of the Spirit, the wisdom of the Spirit, the courage of the Spirit, the love of the Spirit, and so on. Prayer strengthens us as we re-centre ourselves on God's priorities, and as we request the work of his Spirit in our lives.

⌃ Pray

Identify a few worries or problems in your life. Instead of asking God to take them away, work out what aspect of the Spirit's work you need to walk through them, and then ask your Father in heaven to give you the Holy Spirit.

Bible in a year: Genesis 14 • Hebrews 7 • Genesis 15 • Romans 4

Health food

On earth, Jesus did much of his ministry over food. And still today, he has given his church a meal that feeds us—that keeps us healthy and keeps us growing.

Bad manners

Read 1 Corinthians 11:17-22, 27-32

❓ *What is Paul criticising the Corinthian Christians for in v 18 and v 21-22?*

❓ *Why is this serious (v 27-29)?*

Receiving the Lord's Supper without "discerning the body of Christ" (v 29)—that is, without recognising that you do so as part of a church of saved sinners—means you are not eating the Lord's Supper at all (v 20). And it is so important to God that he was willing to discipline these Christians in order that they would not continue down this path towards spiritual shipwreck and eternal condemnation (v 30-32).

Why does it matter so much? Because this meal is a central means by which God strengthens his people. And such strong medicine, when misused, can be fatal.

Visible words

Read 1 Corinthians 11:23-26

Notice the "For" at the start of v 23. Here is the reason that Paul is so firm in the first paragraph of this section.

❓ *Who wants us to share this meal (v 23-25)?*

❓ *What do we remember as we eat bread and drink wine (v 24-25)?*

❓ *What do we look forward to (v 26)?*

The 16th-century Reformer John Calvin called the bread and wine "visible words". God preaches to us through the broken bread and the poured-out wine. As we re-remember the death of Christ, he moves us to appreciate more deeply how we have been brought into his family—why it is we are able to eat at his table both now spiritually and one day physically. Our eating and drinking is a public proclamation of who we are: his children, rescued by his Son's death.

Read 2 Corinthians 3:17-18

We become more like Christ (or, to put it another way, we become healthier Christians) as the Spirit shows us Jesus—as we "see" him. We do this in his word, as we've seen. But we do this in his supper too. As the physical bread and wine enable us spiritually to "see" him on the cross, we are reminded of his love, we are moved to love him, and we are changed to be more like him. And this is why the Lord's Supper is such a wonderful means of strengthening us if we prepare for and receive it rightly—and such a dangerous thing to prepare for flippantly or receive unthinkingly.

⌄ Apply

❓ *How is 1 Corinthians 11:27-29 going to help you prepare for your next sharing of the Lord's Supper?*

❓ *How is verse 26 going to help you know what to think about and pray about as you receive it?*

Church health

In a sense, instead of asking, "How healthy am I, spiritually?" we should ask, "How healthy is my church, spiritually?"

That's because there are very few Christians who are thriving while their church is stagnating or struggling. God saved us to be part of his people; he placed us in a body of his people; and we each grow or shrink spiritually as a member of his people.

That is why, in the New Testament letters, the vast majority are addressed to churches—and the overwhelming majority of those letters' content is aimed at the whole church, not individuals within the church.

Put off, put on

Read Colossians 3:5-14

- ❷ *What must the members of this church "put to death" by ridding themselves of (v 5-10)?*
- ❷ *What must God's chosen people "clothe" themselves with (v 12-14)?*

A Christian who never gave into the sins of v 5-9, and who consistently displayed the virtues of v 12-14, would be an amazing—an extremely Christ like person! But notice how many of both the sins and the qualities are others-focused. Most are flaws and strengths that are displayed in community. And love, the virtue "which binds [the other virtues] all together" (v 14), is relational.

In other words, if we truly want to be spiritually healthy ourselves, we will be committed to the spiritual health of others. The maturity of other members of your church must matter as much to you as your own.

God has given you your church community to help you grow, as you help them grow. Paul goes on to show how we do this...

One another

Read Colossians 3:15-17

- ❷ *What should rule our hearts (v 15)?*

No grudges, no one-upmanship, no divisions. If Christ has made peace with someone, who are we to be in conflict with them?

- ❷ *What should dwell in our hearts (v 16)?*
- ❷ *How does this happen (v 16-17)?*

⌄ Apply

- ❷ *Do you teach and admonish others in your church, based on what you've heard together from the Bible?*
- ❷ *Are you someone who is willing to be taught and admonished themselves?*
- ❷ *Why are we often so slow to do these things for each other, do you think?*

⌃ Pray

Choose three or four people in your church. Pray that they would take off specific sins in verses 5-9 which you know they struggle with, and put on the virtues of verses 12-14. And ask for an opportunity to encourage them.

Christ in creation

The world is set up to enable us to breathe in air that keeps us physically alive. But it is also set up so that we are able to breathe in truth that keeps us spiritually alive.

Read Psalm 19

The ideas of v 7-14—that God's word refreshes us and is precious to us, and that God is our Rock and Redeemer—are fairly familiar. But the psalm doesn't start at v 7!

❷ *What do the heavens, or skies, do all the time (v 1-2)?*

❷ *Since "they use no words" (v 3), in what sense do they do this, do you think?*

Every single aspect of the creation points to its Creator. A snowflake's intricacy, a lightning bolt's power, a cell's complexity, a sunset's beauty. Each tells us there is a Maker, and each tells us something of the Maker. We see his glory reflected in each part of his work that we see around us.

❷ *To what does David compare the sun (v 4-6)?*

In the Old Testament, God describes himself as a bridegroom, with his people as his bride (e.g. Hosea 2:14-23). The Gospels record Jesus using that bridegroom imagery for himself (Mark 2:18-20). And Revelation reveals that when the Lamb, Jesus, returns, it will be to hold a wedding feast for his bride, the church (Revelation 19:7-9), ushering us into a restored world where there will be no need for a sun, "for the glory of God gives it light, and the Lamb is its lamp (21:23).

So when David describes the sun as "a bridegroom" (Psalm 19:5) that gives warmth to all (v 6), he is not just clutching at any old simile. He is saying, *The sun reminds me of you, God—reminds me of your power, your love, your warmth.* And, living after Jesus died to rescue his bride, we can say, *The sun reminds me of you, Jesus—of your power, love and warmth, and of your return, when you will be all the light we need.*

The triune God has painted himself into his creation masterpiece. He made lightning to remind us of the sudden, powerful return of Christ (Luke 17:24). He made snow to show us what he does with our sin (Isaiah 1:18). He made fire to tell us about the power of his purity and the warmth of his Spirit (Exodus 19:18; Acts 2:1-4). He made rocks to enable us to understand his stability (Psalm 19:14). Everywhere in his creation, he is showing us himself.

Remember, spiritual health means becoming more and more like Christ (Romans 8:28-30). We become more and more like Christ as we see more of Christ (2 Corinthians 3:18). And we see Christ throughout his creation, as we learn to look at it with eyes ready to see it "declare the glory of God" (Psalm 19:1).

⌄ Apply

As you go about your day, look for Jesus in his creation. Ask him to point you to himself—who he is and what he's done—in what you see.

The gift of suffering

A healthy Christian is not necessarily a healthy person. A hard truth to grasp is that your suffering is a divine gift to keep you trusting and keep you healthy (spiritually).

Genuine faith

Read 1 Peter 1:3-7

❷ *Because Jesus rose (v 3), what can his people look forward to (v 4)?*

❷ *How do we know we'll get there (v 5)?*

❷ *With what emotion should we respond to this (beginning of v 6)?*

❷ *But what are Peter's readers going through (v 6)?*

❷ *Why have "these ... come" (v 7)?*

Suffering shows what, or who, we really trust in—and what, or who, we find our joy in. Suffering hurts because it involves the removal of a happy circumstance (e.g. a relationship, or a career, or good health, or a secure home). But for the Christian, it does not involve the removal of our joy—because our joy was never primarily found in that thing, but in Christ and our eternal home with him. And so suffering proves the "genuineness of your faith"—not to God (he already knows!) but to you. When we are at our weakest, but we cling on to Christ, we can see that our faith is not fake, but real.

⌄ Apply

❷ *Have you ever experienced a time when you were suffering greatly, and saw that your faith was genuine and your joy was not extinguished? How does that encourage you?*

❷ *Are you suffering right now? How might God be using this suffering to:*
- *show you your faith is genuine?*
- *enable you to locate your joy each day in him, not in circumstances?*
- *make you more like Jesus?*

Run to God

Job is the biblical character whose suffering we see in most detail, and whose response we see at most length. By Job 2:8, Job has lost his wealth, his children, his house and his health—and he has no idea why.

Read Job 2:9-10

❷ *What does Job's wife tell him to do? Why is this understandable?*

I have not suffered as Job and his wife did. But I have certainly had the same reaction as Job's wife in my mind.

❷ *How does Job respond (v 10)?*

In suffering, we either run away from God in despair and bitterness, or towards God in desperate trust. The first is easier; the second is greater. It assures us of our faith and of our future, and means that we are joyful, not crushed.

⌃ Pray

❷ *How do you need to pray for yourself in light of these truths?*

❷ *Who else do you need to pray for?*

The route to blessing #2

The first step to blessing, as we saw last Sunday, is to "repent". The second is to "believe".

Delight

Read Psalm 1

> ❷ *What do you think it means to "delight ... in the law of the LORD" (v 2)?*

At first sight this may seem a little weird. Perhaps it conjures up an image of people who obsess about rules, and take delight in pointing out how others fail them. The worst caricature of a Christian, in fact. But that misses the point.

The "law" refers to the first five books of our Bible, which are the story of God's dealing with mankind, and his choosing and blessing of the people of Israel. The "rules" of godly living (e.g. the Ten Commandments) are about our grateful and dutiful response to the God who saves us. And notice how personal it is: "his law" as well as "the law". It is the expression of the character and purposes of a personal God who relates to me personally.

···· TIME OUT ·····································

Read Exodus 20:1-3

Verse 2 is key to understanding the commandments. They are not rules to live by to find the blessing of God. They are the way to please the God who has already blessed you.

⌄ Apply

The first readers would have delighted in the way God had rescued them from Egypt so they could live his way as his people. Now we are to delight in the gospel of Christ—at the way he has rescued us from sin and death, so we can enjoy living his way as his people for ever.

> ❷ *Think about what you take most delight in. How does the gospel compare?*
> ❷ *How can you delight more in who Jesus is, and in living for him?*

One answer to that is coming up now!

Meditate

> ❷ *What do you think it might mean to meditate on God's law "day and night"?*
> ❷ *How is that different from the "sinners" of Psalm 1:1?*

The gospel should be what drives us, not the advice of others or the way the world works, or even what *we* think. The gospel is what delivers to us the blessing of God— true happiness. It is the thing that we must come back to all the time when we are deciding what to think or how to live.

⌃ Pray

Talk to God about the gospel. Delight in him; delight in what he has done for you. And ask God to prompt you to think about the gospel constantly, day and night, so that it would remove any other influence that would rob you of your blessing.

The family doctor

It is one thing to recognise where we are struggling, and how God is working in that to grow our faith; it is quite another thing to actually change.

In fact, it is impossible for us to do that. Which is why it is wonderful that God has given us someone to enable us to make those changes. And that person is—himself: his Spirit.

If you want to be a healthy, thriving Christian, you will need to put effort in (2 Peter 1:5, 10). But you will need to make that effort while relying on God's Spirit to take that effort and use it to change you. To put it another way, the Spirit is the doctor who applies the God-given vitamins to our spiritual lives. We're going to take three studies to see how the Spirit is working in you.

Birth

Read John 3:3-8

> ❷ *How does someone become part of God's kingdom, enjoying new life (v 3, 5-6)?*

The Spirit is the midwife of our eternal lives. Without his work, you would not be a follower of Jesus. "No one can say, 'Jesus is Lord,' except by the Holy Spirit" (1 Corinthians 12:3).

Family

Read Romans 8:10-17

> ❷ *If we have the Spirit (that is, if we know Jesus as our Lord)...*
> - *what can we look forward to (v 11)?*
> - *what will we seek to do (v 12-13)?*
> - *who are we (v 14)?*

> ❷ *What are the implications of having been "born again" into God's family (v 15-17)?*

Part of the Spirit's work in God's people is to assure them of who they are, enable them to experience the joy of who they are, and help them to live as who they are. The more confident we are that we "are the children of God ... heirs of God and co-heirs with Christ" (v 14, 17), the more we will enjoy that status and the intimacy with our Creator God that it brings (v 15). And the more we enjoy being children of God, the more we'll want to "put to death the misdeeds of the body" (v 13), which is our obligation to our new Father and our new family. And even as we seek to do this, we find that it is "by the Spirit" that we are enabled to do it (v 13).

⌄ Apply

> ❷ *Do you struggle for assurance of your status? Will you ask the Spirit daily to remind you that you are a child of God?*

> ❷ *Do you struggle for enjoyment of your status? How will you "cry, 'Abba, Father'" and how will you remind yourself of your glorious inheritance?*

> ❷ *Do you struggle to live out your status? What "misdeeds of the body" do you need to ask the Spirit to enable you to stop playing with, and instead put to death?*

The grower of fruit

Letting the Spirit do his work in us is not easy—because in a very real sense, we don't want him to do it.

Read Galatians 5:15-26

The battle

❓ *What does Paul say will not happen if and as we "live by the Spirit" (v 16)?*

The "flesh" is our "sinful nature" (NIV84)— our old selves, which were ruled by sin.

❓ *What is the relationship between the Spirit living in us and our old selves clinging to us (v 17)?*

If you feel that living as a Christian is a constant battle within, be encouraged—that's what truly living as a Christian involves! It's only if we feel there is no battle that we should be concerned, because that means our flesh is winning.

❓ *How do verses 18 and 25 tell us what it means to "live by the Spirit"?*

In verse 18, Paul is contrasting two motivations for obeying God—the Spirit and being "under the law". The Spirit motivates us by reminding us of our Spirit-given identity— children of God (Romans 8). Living "under the law" means we are driven by earning our identity—so we're motivated by pride (because we're better than others) or fear (because we're terrified God might reject us). So living "under the law" can therefore never produce fruit such as peace or lack of conceit and envy (Galatians 5:22, 26).

The growth

❓ *Which "acts of the flesh" (v 19-21) are you battling, or being defeated by?*

❓ *Which parts of the "fruit of the Spirit" (v 22-23) do you see growing in your life? Which feel most distant from you?*

Verse 24 reminds us of what has happened to our old, sinful selves—our "flesh": it has been crucified. When Christ died, it died— the penalty for it was taken and its power over us was broken. But its pull remains— so we need to keep killing what has been crucified. And we do this by keeping "in step with the Spirit" (v 25). He strengthens us to say "no" to our flesh, and as we do this, he grows in us his fruit. Our job is to let the Spirit do his job.

🔼 Pray

Identify the acts of the flesh you most struggle with, and ask the Spirit to help you want to live as a child of God when you feel that tug.

Identify the parts of the fruit of the Spirit you most struggle to grow, and commit to working with the Spirit to enable those virtues to grow in you.

Finally, pray for your church. The "you" in these verses is plural—you will crucify the flesh and grow this fruit as part of your church. So pray these things for your church, as well as for yourself.

Bible in a year: Luke 3, Luke 16 • Genesis 24 – 25

The giver of gifts

Healthy Christians are serving Christians, because the Spirit works in us to work through us to help God's people.

God's gifts

Read 1 Corinthians 12:1-11

- ❓ *Why are you good at particular things (v 4-6)?*
- ❓ *For what purpose are you good at those things (v 7)?*

The list in v 8-11 is not exhaustive. Paul gives a flavour of the gifts, so that we can see that they come in great variety, but from one source (v 11), and for one purpose—the common good of God's people (v 7).

Apply

Your talents are not *from* you, and your talents are not *for* you.

- ❓ *Does this truth mean you need to change your view of your abilities in any way?*
- ❓ *Is there anything you need to speak to a church leader about, e.g. offering your services to your church?*

Church body

Read 1 Corinthians 12:12-31

Paul is using the image of a body to describe your local church—and your part in it.

- ❓ *What point is he making about your place in your church in:*
  - *v 15-20?* • *v 21-25?* • *v 26?*

Pray

Ask God, by his Spirit, to give you a right view of yourself and your church—neither thinking you have nothing to offer others, nor that you have no need of others. Ask for such an identification with your church that you suffer when another member does, and feel joy when another is honoured.

The most excellent way

Read 1 Corinthians 13:1-7

- ❓ *What kind of very godly-looking actions are potentially useless (v 1-3)? Why?*
- ❓ *Why does this mean you could apply chapter 12 perfectly, and uselessly?*

Part of my problem when it comes to my spiritual health: *I just don't love others very much*. That's why I use my Spirit-given gifts in my time, for my own sake; or only use them for others in a grudging, is-this-enough-now way or a proud, I-hope-people-notice way. Maybe you're similar. Thankfully, as we've seen, we don't have to look inside ourselves to summon up the kind of love Paul describes in v 4-7. We look to the Father, who out of love sent his Son; to the Son, who out of love went to the cross; and to the Spirit, who grows his fruit in us—the first part of which is love (Galatians 5:22).

A healthy Christian is a serving Christian and a loving Christian. And that is what the Spirit is working to make you.

Bible in a year: John 8 • Obadiah • Psalm 81 • Malachi 1

EZEKIEL: In exile

Imagine living in a time of economic uncertainty, international upheaval, institutional corruption, a self-centred population, and rejection of God's word.

Sound familiar?! This describes the time of Ezekiel, the prophet who preached to Israelites in Babylonian exile. The year is 593 BC; God's people, Judah, have been conquered and many have been relocated to a foreign land. What does God want to say to his people?

A humbling situation

Read Ezekiel 1:1-3

❷ *Where was Ezekiel, and what did he see (v 1)?*

❷ *Who was in exile (v 2)? How do you think a citizen of Judah such as Ezekiel would feel about this?*

Psalm 137:1 best captures the mood of the exiles: "By the rivers of Babylon we sat and wept when we remembered Zion". They had lost their homes and their place of worship, and they appeared to be without the hope of a victorious king. Why? "It was because of the LORD's anger that all this happened to Jerusalem and Judah, and in the end he thrust them from his presence" (2 Kings 24:20).

The king is in exile, defeated and powerless. Yet there is another King, who is still seated on his throne...

⌄ Apply

Our sins should exclude us from God's presence, eternally. So our lives should be marked by godly sorrow—Jesus says: "Blessed are those who mourn, for they will be comforted" (Matthew 5:4). If we want comfort from the guilt of our sin, we must first be grieved by it.

❷ *Do you really grieve over your sin? Why not do so now?*

A humbling encounter

Read Ezekiel 1:4-28

❷ *What picture of God do you get from the vision he gives Ezekiel?*

❷ *What effect is the vision designed to have, do you think?*

❷ *What is Ezekiel's response (v 28)?*

The wheels symbolise mobility and omnipresence. The living creatures represent the intelligence (a man), royalty (lion), strength (bull), and compassion (eagle—see Exodus 19:4) of God. The closer the vision gets to God, the more difficult it is for Ezekiel to describe it.

⌄ Apply

The more we grasp the awesomeness of God, the more we will worship him.

❷ *What has particularly struck you about this vision of God? Why?*

❷ *How will that prompt you to worship him today?*

Eating his words

God's word is a precious thing to his people. But it is not a comfortable thing.

A tough audience

Read Ezekiel 2:1-5; 3:4-7

- *What task does God give to Ezekiel in these sections?*
- *How are the people he'll be speaking to described?*
- *Why won't they listen (2:4; 3:7)?*

A tough prophet

Read Ezekiel 2:6-8; 3:8-17

Ezekiel is not to be afraid, despite the reception his message will receive (2:6-7).

- *What does God command him to do instead (v 8)?*

This prophet is going to need a thick skin (3:8-9). He will need to be hardened to rejection and suffering. But this hardness will be a hardness to rebellion, rather than a hardness in rebellion. It is good to be stubborn, when we are stubborn about holding to God's word!

Apply

- *In what ways do you find yourself being stubborn about listening to and obeying God's word? How do you need to become less stubborn?*
- *Are there times you need to be more stubborn about holding to God's word?*

A tough assignment

Read Ezekiel 3:18-27

- *What is Ezekiel responsible for, and not responsible for?*
- *How would this have both challenged and liberated him as he began to speak for God?*

Apart from when God is speaking through him, Ezekiel will be made silent (v 26-27). All his words will be God's words.

Apply

- *What makes you afraid of speaking to others about God?*
- *What difference will it make to you this week to remember that you are responsible for warning others about God's standards and judgment; but that you are not responsible for their response?*

A sweet truth

Read Ezekiel 2:9 – 3:3

Ezekiel is given a scroll with God's words on it. He is to eat it, as a sign that God's words bring spiritual life, just as bread gives physical life (see Matthew 4:4). God's word can expose our hearts and challenge how we live. But it is also sweet, and deeply satisfying. Thank God that you're reading it now!

This is not comfortable

Ezekiel is in exile in Babylon, and Judah has been occupied; but Jerusalem, the capital, is holding out. God calls Ezekiel to act out what will happen to Jerusalem.

This is a very long section, so we will focus on particular parts of it.

Sin's pain

Read Ezekiel 4:1-17

Ezekiel symbolises Israel's long history of accumulated sin on this bed of sorrows where he "bears" the sins of the people. "390 days" represents the years that the nation of Israel had spent sinning. "40 days" represents the years of exile which they now have to face.

···· TIME OUT ·······································

There may also be some hope in these numbers. 40 days/years is reminiscent of the exodus generation spending 40 years in the desert for their sin. But after that, the people entered the land. And 390 plus 40 equals 430, which was the number of years Israel spent in Egypt before God rescued them. These numbers are about God's judgment of his people; but they also seem to point to a new "exodus" and "promised land" beyond the exile.

···

❓ *Imagine you are an exile walking past Ezekiel as he enacts this. How should you feel, do you think?*

Sin's offence

Read Ezekiel 5:5-11

❓ *Why will God do this to Jerusalem (v 5-8, 11)?*

Sin's judgment

Read Ezekiel 6:4-6

❓ *What do these verses tell us about Israel's religion?*

❓ *What will happen as God judges this?*

Read Ezekiel 7:1-4

❓ *How would you describe the scope of the judgment?*

Read Ezekiel 7:16-27

❓ *What, and who, will be unable to help them?*

In verse 27, God promises that: "I will deal with them according to their conduct". God's anger is not uncontrolled or unfair. His judgment is in proportion to the sin committed. When we find the idea of God's wrath too difficult or even unpalatable, it is because we are treating sin too lightly.

⌄ Apply

❓ *How does this view of God's wrath make you feel about your own sin?*

❓ *How does it impact your appreciation of Christ's sin-bearing death?*

The mark of the blessed

How do you spot someone who is truly blessed by God?

❓ *What is the quality you most look for in friends, work colleagues or yourself?*

There may be many things—good humour, professionalism, truthfulness. Did you have words like faithfulness and reliability somewhere on your list? Whatever their character, if an acquaintance is faithful and not flighty, constant not capricious, then they are someone you can trust and depend on.

Read Psalm 1:3

Think about the image of a tree being used here.

❓ *Why is the tree "evergreen", do you think?*

❓ *What are the visible results of its invisible source of nourishment?*

A Christian shows constancy, or stickability, because he or she has built his life on Christ, who is the same yesterday, today and for ever (Hebrews 13:8). As our life grows in us by the Holy Spirit's work in our hearts, we start to show the same qualities in our lives as Jesus did in his. We are not blown about by popular or clever-sounding opinions. We are not dragged off course by friends or enemies. We do not seek to feel better about ourselves, or gain recognition for ourselves, by pushing others down.

···· TIME OUT ···

Is the end of Psalm 1:3 a promise that Christians close to God will grow rich? Yes—and no! In the Old Testament God illustrated with worldly wealth the blessing he poured out on those he loved. But this is an illustration only. Some believers will enjoy the blessing and responsibility of worldly wealth. Others will enjoy the blessing and responsibility of worldly poverty. We are all rich beyond our wildest dreams in Christ.

Read Ephesians 2:7 and 3:8

⌄ Apply

Is Psalm 1:3 a picture of the person you want to be? The clues to how to get there are in the image. Plant yourself in Christ. Draw your strength and sustenance from him. Meditate day and night on the gospel of God, and you will grow more like Christ by the grace and power of God.

❓ *As you look forward to the next week, at what time do you think you will be in most danger of forgetting about the gospel? What will you do at that point to remind yourself?*

⌃ Pray

Speak to God about verse 3 now. Ask him to establish you in Christ so that you will be evergreen, fruitful, and wealthy in the only way that matters; and so that you will be a blessing to others.

No trivial matter

Ezekiel is about to have a visionary tour of Jerusalem. But it's not a reel of tourists' highlights. It's a much more depressing tour.

Exposed

Read Ezekiel 8:1-18

- ❷ *What locations are being used to worship idols? Why is this shocking?*
- ❷ *Who is leading this idol-worship (v 10-11)? What do they think about the real God (v 12)?*

Tammuz (v 14) was the Sumerian god of vegetation. The wilting of the vegetation each year was seen as a sign of his death, hence the weeping. Jaazaniah, the son of Shaphan, is picked out in verse 11 because his family had a long and distinguished history of loyalty to God (see 2 Kings 22:8-10; Jeremiah 26:24). The point is: if even this family is worshipping idols in the heart of God's place in God's city, then there is no hope.

- ❷ *What is the right answer to the second question in Ezekiel 8:17?*

Apply

We all have hearts which love to worship things that are not God—idols.

- ❷ *What are the three idols you most struggle not to love more than God?*
- ❷ *Do you see your over-devotion to them as trivial?*
- ❷ *How does verse 18 challenge you?*

Pray

Presumably, most visitors to Jerusalem would have noticed the walls, the temple, the palaces—but not the idols. It takes a tour which includes God's commentary to show us what is really going on.

Pray that God would give you a similar insight into your own thoughts, feelings and actions, so you can see your idols.

Destroyed

Read Ezekiel 9:1-11

- ❷ *What does God begin to arrange (v 1-2)?*
- ❷ *Who gets the "mark" (v 4)? Why is this crucial (v 5-6)?*
- ❷ *What is Ezekiel's response (v 8)?*

The saving mark comes up again in Revelation 9:4, and is also referred to as the seal of the Holy Spirit (Ephesians 1:13-14). Again, we see the justice of God's judgment. He will "bring down on their own heads what they have done" (Ezekiel 9:10). Idolatry—treating God as less important or lovely than something he has made—is not trivial.

Pray

Thank God that he marks people for salvation from his judgment. Thank him that the mark is not given to those who are perfect, but to those who grieve over the imperfections of their lives and their society.

Goodbye God

What is the worst thing that can happen to a city; a church; a person?

Chapters 10 and 11 are a part of the vision in chapters 8 and 9.

Departing

Read Ezekiel 10:1-22

The temple was the place where God dwelled among his people. It was where Israel could come and meet with, worship, and find guidance from God. It was the place where, through sacrifice, forgiveness was available. It was the most important place in God's city, God's land, God's world.

❷ *What does Ezekiel see and hear (v 1-5)?*

❷ *Where is God moving from (v 4, 15-19)?*

❷ *Why does this matter?*

Cherubim are spiritual servants who worship God and proclaim his holiness (see Exodus 25:18-22). The throne symbolises God's power and rule.

Condemning

Read Ezekiel 11:1-15

❷ *What were the leaders guilty of (v 1-2, 6)?*

❷ *What did they (wrongly) assume (v 3)?*

❷ *Whose example had they followed (v 12)?*

And so the leaders face judgment (v 8-9). The tragedy is that the leaders of God's people will only really understand that the Lord is God when they face his anger (v 12).

The people in Jerusalem thought of themselves as meat in a cooking pot (v 3). That is, they were the choice people, left behind when the first exiles were taken to Babylon. They thought they were safe. But God says: *I will take you out of your safety and you will face judgment.* And later, in chapter 24, he will use the image of the cooking pot itself, but in a very different way.

Returning

Read Ezekiel 11:16-25

The sanctuary had been the Jerusalem Temple. Now God had left it, and his people were scattered.

❷ *So what is he saying in verse 16? Why would this have been wonderfully reassuring?*

❷ *What does God promise about the future? (v 17; v 18; v 19-20)*

This great return will finally happen when Jesus, who has sent his Spirit into his people to turn their hearts away from idol-worship and towards loving obedience, returns to gather his people and live with them (see Mark 13:26-27).

⌃ Pray

Thank God for sending Jesus to die for your sin and bring you into his people. Thank him that one day his Son will return to gather you to himself.

The lesson in digging

Often people are surprised that they are sinners. We can see others' sins; but we tend to be much poorer at noticing our own.

A rebellious people

Read Ezekiel 12:1-3

❓ *What do these people have, and what do they not have (v 2)?*

❓ *How are they described as a whole (v 3)?*

It is striking that these exiles are still characterised by rebellion. They can apply truth to others, but not to themselves. They are blind to their blindness.

···· TIME OUT ·······································

Jesus said we actually want to be blind, to live in darkness. God's truth is like light piercing the darkness of the lives we've chosen for ourselves. **Read John 3:19-20**. And we can't choose to see the light on our own—**read 1 Corinthians 2:14**.

Pray for eyes to see yourself rightly: to notice your sin, and then to repent of it rather than excusing it.

An obedient prophet

Read Ezekiel 12:4-7

❓ *What must Ezekiel do:*
  • *in the daytime?*
  • *in the evening?*

Six times in verses 4-7 we read about Ezekiel's audience "watching" him. Ezekiel feared God, not what others thought of him.

⌄ Apply

❓ *When does the good opinion of others direct the way you behave?*

❓ *What impact does being thought well of by others have on your witness to them?*

❓ *When, and how, do you need to be like Ezekiel in verse 7, and do as you are commanded?*

Certain destruction

Read Ezekiel 12:8-20

❓ *What will happen to:*
  • *the prince (v 12-14)?*
  • *the people left behind (v 18-20)?*

Now we see that Ezekiel is acting out what the king in Jerusalem will do for real: **read 2 Kings 25:1-7**.

When God judges, "they will know that I am the LORD" (Ezekiel 12:15, 16, 20). If only they would recognise him as Lord now, before it is too late, when repentance is possible and salvation is on offer.

⌄ Apply

"Now is the day of salvation" (2 Corinthians 6:2).

❓ *How does this encourage you to tell others about the Lord?*

❓ *Are you delaying obeying God in any way? How will you change?*

Bible in a year: Genesis 37 – 40

False teachers are losers

Not every teacher was as pessimistic about Jerusalem's future as Ezekiel was. And after all, Ezekiel was pretty extreme in his message. Others were much more moderate.

Read Ezekiel 12:21 – 13:23

False sayings

❓ *What were other prophets saying?*

- 12:22 • 13:7 • 13:10

❓ *What were they saying specifically about Ezekiel's claims (12:27)?*

Divination is observing natural phenomena to explain the spiritual realm and predict the future.

···· TIME OUT ··

Ezekiel's day was hardly unique.

Read 2 Peter 3:3-4

❓ *Are you ever tempted to think like this? Why is it tempting?*

⏶ Pray

Praise God for his patience in not yet returning to bring final judgment. Ask him to help you use this time not to doubt his word, but to spread it.

False teachers

❓ *What motivated these teachers (Ezekiel 13:19)?*

❓ *Where did their "revelations" come from (v 2, 17)?*

❓ *What does God liken them to (v 3-4)? What point is he making, do you think?*

Like stonemasons who covered major breaks in the wall by applying whitewash instead of repairing the real problem (v 5, 10-11), these false teachers refuse to speak the truth about the reality of sin, the coming of judgment, and the need for humble repentance.

⏷ Apply

❓ *Why is false teaching so attractive, do you think?*

❓ *What are the areas and repeated actions in your life where you'd like to hear someone say, "God doesn't really mind about that" or "Let's not be negative; it's a normal part of life"?*

Those are the areas where you're most susceptible to false teaching!

Faithful God

❓ *What is going to happen, does God say (12:23-28)?*

❓ *What will happen to the false prophets (13:3, 8-9)?*

❓ *What does God promise the faithful few (v 23)?*

⏶ Pray

Pray for your church leader(s), that they will preach and teach not what people want to hear, but what God wants people to hear.

True loyalties exposed

To repent means to change allegiances. Believers are people who agree with God about their sin and therefore take action against it.

Secret idolatry

Read Ezekiel 14:1-8

- ❓ *What is shocking about the God-given insight Ezekiel has about these visitors (v 1-3)?*
- ❓ *What do they need to do (v 6)?*
- ❓ *What does God do when his people start worshipping idols (v 4-5, 8)?*

If we belong to his people, God's treatment of our idolatry is loving. As long as we love other things and yet are blessed by God, we can believe our idols are blessing us. The removal of his blessing shows us who the real God is. We need to avoid being like these elders—what Jesus called hypocrites, and what James would call "double-minded" (see James 1:2-8).

···· TIME OUT ·····································

- ❓ *Of what idols do you need to hear the challenge of Ezekiel 14:6?*
- ❓ *What would it look like for you to repent—turn away from and remove your allegiance from—those idols?*

Deception allowed

Read Ezekiel 14:9-23

Verses 9-10 are talking of false prophets.

- ❓ *How does God judge Israel through their ministry (v 9-10)?*

One way God judges is in giving people exactly what they have chosen. If we want to be told lies about who God is so that we can live however we want, then God will let us listen to liars. Ezekiel is not ascribing evil to God. He is saying that God can use evil as a means to judge. God rules over hearts.

⌃ Pray

Sometimes, getting what our hearts desire is the worst thing that can happen to us. So pray that God would not give you what you want, but what he knows you need. Thank him for giving you his Spirit, to work in your heart and change your desires (see Luke 11:11-13).

- ❓ *What point is God making, and repeating, as he mentions the hypothetical presence of three godly men in various places (Ezekiel 14:12-19)?*

God's point in v 21-23 is that he will judge the ungodly, and save the repentant. When the exiles meet those who were rescued, they'll understand that God judges fairly because he has saved those who did repent and turn back to him.

⌃ Pray

It is worth remembering that the presence of godly people does not save those who know them. Pray now for any family members or friends who do not know Jesus themselves. They do need to repent!

The lesson of the vine

Israel was created by God to live for and display his glory. But since they haven't done this, what is Israel useful for?

A pointless vine

Read Ezekiel 15:1-5

- ❓ *What kind of plant is Israel likened to?*
- ❓ *What is the only purpose it has (v 2-3)?*
- ❓ *What makes it even more useless (v 4-5)?*

The image of Israel as a vine is not unique to Ezekiel (if you have time, look up Hosea 10:1; Isaiah 5:1-2 and Psalm 80:8-15). Like a very large vine, Israel was to fill the earth with fruit; the fruit of obedient worship.

Humanity has been failing to live out its God-given purposes for a long time. Adam and Eve failed to carry out their role as royal-image-bearers, just as Israel failed to act as God's representatives on earth, not showing the nations the fruitfulness of living with him as King.

Read Psalm 80:14-17

Here is the true vine, the only hope for humanity, which is (strangely) raised up by God, then cut down, and then raised up again. This is the man who called himself "the true vine" (John 15:1). Here is the new Adam, and the true Israel.

···· TIME OUT ························

Read John 15:1-9

- ❓ *What role do Christians have in the new, true vine (v 4-5)?*

- ❓ *How does verse 7 show us what it means in reality to remain attached to the vine of Jesus?*

A burned vine

Read Ezekiel 15:6-8

As God speaks through Ezekiel, the coming of the true vine still lies in the future...

- ❓ *What will God do to this useless vine (v 6)?*

Israel has tasted fire before, in slavery in Egypt. But they will taste it again because of their unfaithfulness. The land God gave them will be infertile, useless for growing vines.

Jerusalem has failed, and Jerusalem will fall—burned like a useless vine. Jesus never failed, yet he too was "burned"— not for his own disobedience, but for his people's. God set his face against his own Son, and then raised him up to be the eternal vine. Ezekiel 15 is pointing us forwards to Christ!

⌃ Pray

Thank God for the ultimate vine—the true Israel. Thank him that Jesus bore the fire of judgment for you, and has grafted you into his vine. Pray that you would grow fruit, to his glory.

Wages of wickedness

In the second half of this song, we are introduced to another great theme of the psalms: the ruin of those who reject God.

Read Psalm 1

Incredible disappearance

The signs of the person blessed by God are growth, endurance and fruitfulness (v 3).

> ❷ *What is the only reality about the wicked that really matters, according to verse 4?*

The wicked have no future. Like an insignificant by-product from a factory that's simply dumped. Or like the husks from the wheat, which are just an annoyance to the farmer. In the end their lives are worth nothing; the wind blows and they are gone.

···· TIME OUT ·······································

> ❷ *Do you struggle to believe that this is truly the way of things?*

The wicked dominate the news headlines every day. They seem so big, so permanent, so important and influential. By contrast, the humble, struggling believer seems so insignificant. But the eye of faith sees that, in God's value system, the opposite is true. It is sometimes hard to believe this—but it's something the writers of the psalms recognise and continually remind us of.

Read Psalm 73:1-20

Terrifying judgment

The blessed man looks to a new day coming when God's judgment will make the distinction clear for all to see. There will be no reprieve for the wicked on that day. No last-minute second chance. No place among God's people for those who have spent their lives mocking God's gospel.

> ❷ *Is this how you see your non-Christian friends and family? Even the "nice" ones?*

It's very easy to deceive ourselves on this issue. Our family, our closest mates, our beloved spouse even—all are facing the wrath of God's holy judgment if they have chosen to defy him.

🔽 Apply

Think about those people now.

> ❷ *How are you showing them what it is like to enjoy the blessing of life under God's rule?*

> ❷ *How, and when, might you be able to speak to them about how they might be blessed, and not blown away?*

The God who will judge sent his Son to take that judgment. Ask him to work in the hearts of those you love but who don't love God, so that they won't have to endure his anger, but can enjoy his blessing.

The prostitute who pays

Sin is deeply offensive to God, in the same way that infidelity is to husbands and wives. Though much of this chapter is specific to Israel, in general it applies to all sinners.

What God did

Read Ezekiel 16:1-14

❓ *What was Jerusalem's background before and shortly after "birth" (v 3-5)?*

❓ *What happened next (v 6-7)?*

❓ *And after that (v 8-14)?*

TIME OUT

In some ways, this is analogous to our story as Christians.

Read Ephesians 2:1-10 and Revelation 21:2-4

❓ *What state were we in before God rescued us?*

❓ *How do these passages both keep us humble and increase our love for our Lord?*

God has been his people's midwife, mother and husband. Everything they have, are and enjoy is a gift from him. Which is what makes what comes next so shocking...

What Jerusalem did

Read Ezekiel 16:15-52

❓ *What has Jerusalem used God's gifts to do (v 15-22)?*

❓ *What has she done with her children (v 20-21)?*

Verses 33-34 are perhaps particularly shocking. Sin is spending all we have on being spiritually adulterous to God.

Sodom as well as Samaria (the capital of the northern kingdom of God's people, which had already been destroyed by this stage) were notorious for their sinfulness, and had faced God's judgment.

❓ *So what point is God making in verses 43-52?*

What God will do

Read Ezekiel 16:53-63

Punishment must, and will, come (v 58-59). Yet...

❓ *What will God do (v 60, 62)?*

❓ *What will God have to do in order to restore his relationship with his people (v 63)?*

God will both punish his people's sin, and have mercy on his people. How can he do both? Verse 63 hints at it—he will have to atone for their sin. The jilted Lover will be the forgiving Husband, by taking on himself the punishment his bride deserves.

☑ Apply

❓ *How are you going to think and act differently in light of Ezekiel 16?*

❓ *How does this chapter show you the magnitude of what God did at the cross?*

Eagles, cedars and vines

This chapter presents us with another allegory, about two birds and two plants. This one comes with an explanation.

Read Ezekiel 17:1-24

Two eagles, one vine

- ❓ *Using verses 3-4 and 12-14, who is the eagle, and who is the "top of a cedar"?*
- ❓ *Using verses 7-8 and 15, who is the second eagle, and what does the vine's response to it represent?*

Broken covenant

Though the exile was a catastrophe, it did also have a redemptive purpose. God had ensured that his exiled people would live in a place where they could survive, and even in some ways thrive (v 8). The cedar of Lebanon (which, slightly confusingly, turns into a vine) represents Israel's Davidic kingship (see 1 Kings 7:2; Jeremiah 22:23). But instead of humbly recognising God's hand in bringing the kingdom low (Ezekiel 17:14), King Zedekiah turned his back on the covenant he had made with Babylon, turning to the Pharaoh of Egypt.

- ❓ *What will happen to Zedekiah's bid for independence (v 16-17)?*

Zedekiah tried to go around God's plan and be the saviour of Israel so that he could be the ruler of it. It won't work; and the consequences will be catastrophic (v 19-21).

A new cedar

- ❓ *What is God going to do, and where (v 22-23)?*
- ❓ *What will all the other "trees" (i.e. nations) then learn (v 24)?*

The "birds" also represent other nations. There will be those outside the Jewish people who not only know that their God is the true God but come to join his people (v 23).

Read Mark 4:30-32

- ❓ *Where is this tree to be found?*

Zedekiah was a covenant-breaker, but God is a covenant-keeper. The Father had promised to give his people an eternal Davidic King, and in sending his Son, he kept his word. And the Son lived a life of perfect covenant obedience to his Father. Here is the ultimate Davidic King: God himself, come to save and rule his people.

⌃ Pray

Give thanks that Jesus is the great covenant-keeping King who can completely save and perfectly rule people. Thank him for your place in his kingdom, and that his kingdom is open to all.

Tell him about any parts of your life where you are tempted to ignore his word and seek blessing elsewhere. Pray that he would help you to know the blessing of living with him as King in those areas.

Sin = die; repent = live

Here is a chapter with a very simple headline!

The wrong proverb

Read Ezekiel 18:1-4

❓ *According to the proverb, what happens when a father eats sour grapes (v 2)?*

❓ *If you substitute "sin" for "grapes", what is the meaning of the proverb?*

❓ *What does God think of it (v 3)?!*

In two senses, the proverb is true. The misdeeds of one generation are felt by the next. And we are all born sinful—we "inherit" that from our first father, Adam (see Romans 5:12). But in Ezekiel's time, the current generation is blaming all their suffering on the sins of the previous one.

❓ *Whose sin do you die for, though (Ezekiel 18:4)?*

···· TIME OUT ··································

❓ *Why is blaming flaws and failures on others so attractive to us, do you think?*

❓ *What are the excuses for sin people use in your culture and community?*

❓ *Which ones do you find yourself using?*

The right man

Read Ezekiel 18:4-9

❓ *What does the Lord declare about the man of verses 5-9 (v 9)?*

⌄ Apply

❓ *To what extent do these verses describe you?*

❓ *Which of these verses encourage you; which of them challenge you?*

❓ *What changes do you need to make to be more like this "righteous" man?*

Read Ezekiel 18:10-32

❓ *What does this man's son do (v 10-13)? With what result (v 13)?*

❓ *What does this second man's son do (v 14-17)? With what result (v 17)?*

The point is pretty clear: you are responsible for your own attitudes and actions. It's summed up in verses 25-28. Turn from sin, stop your sin, act rightly, and you'll live.

❓ *What do we need in order to do that (v 31)?*

This is just. But it leaves us with a problem. We haven't lived rightly, constantly. We don't manage to turn completely from our sin. And no one can "get a new heart". We have no righteousness to be "credited" to our account.

Read 2 Corinthians 5:21

❓ *Why is this verse such good news?*

We can be perfectly righteous—by asking Jesus to give us his perfection. If you have never done this, "repent and live!" (Ezekiel 18:32). If you have, thank him for his gift.

Your mother was a...

Who, or what, rules your life? Or, to put it another way: what do you look to for help in difficult times? What do you think about to reassure you that things will be ok?

... Lioness

Read Ezekiel 19:1-9

❓ *What is the mood of the passage (v 1)?*

❓ *How does this mother-lioness compare to the other lions (v 2)?*

❓ *What happened to:*
  • *her first cub (v 3-4)?*
  • *her second cub (v 5-9)?*

A lament is a funeral poem or song. But instead of listing the virtues of the departed kings (or princes), it lists the faults. The two cubs are King Jehoahaz (who was taken to Egypt, 2 Kings 23:31-35), and King Jehoiachin (taken to Babylon, 2 Kings 24:12). Jerusalem is kingless and therefore hopeless. The lament serves to remind them that there will be no more chances. The lament is given to put to death false optimism and an arrogant sense of entitlement. Any expectation of a king is sadly gone now.

... Vine

Read Ezekiel 19:10-14

The vine is a picture of blessing: fruitful, watered, impressive and ruled (v 10-11).

❓ *What happened to this vine (v 12)?*

❓ *Where did that wind come from (v 12)?*

❓ *Where is the vine now, and what can it no longer do (v 13-14)?*

The east wind represents the Babylonian captivity. No branches "fit for a ruler's sceptre" means no victorious king in the near future. In Genesis 49:8-12, God had promised his people a lion-cub-like, sceptre-holding ruler from the tribe of Judah. But now there are no lion cubs, and no sceptre.

···· TIME OUT ·····································

Read Revelation 5:5-6

We can look back now, and see that the King—the Lion of Judah—came to earth to live, die and rise, and then ascended to rule on the throne of heaven.

✓ Apply

In reality, we all have a ruler. The question is—is it the Lion of Judah, or someone/something else?

❓ *Look back to today's sub-heading introduction. Is your answer to those questions "the Lord Jesus"? What difference would it make if it were?*

⌃ Pray

The Lord took away the princes of Israel so that the people would know the lament of life without rule, and look towards the Ruler. It's a challenging thing to pray, but ask God to remove anything in your life which is ruling you, so that you are able to enjoy the rescue and rule of the Lion of Judah.

The good old days?

If you have not been following Jesus all your life, how do you look back on the days before you knew Christ as your Lord?

These verses challenge Israel, and us, to see ourselves rightly.

Rebellion recounted

Read Ezekiel 20:1-29

The elders of Israel come to enquire of God (v 1-3). And he doesn't let them (v 3). Instead, he tells Ezekiel to "confront them" with a history lesson (v 4).

- ❓ *What had God done for them (v 5-6)? What had he asked of them (v 7)?*
- ❓ *What did Israel do (v 8-9, 13, 21)?*
- ❓ *How does God respond each time, in:*
  - • *v 9-12?* • *v 13-20?* • *v 21-26?*

Verses 27-29 are a summary of the history of Israel's performance once they had reached the land. They bring the history lesson right up to the present-day exile.

···· TIME OUT ··························

Notice that God saves his rebellious people for the sake of his own name (v 9, 14, 22). He had promised to bless them in the land; his reputation was at stake. Our salvation, too, is not so much for our sake, but for God's. And it is not for our glory, but for his.

⌄ Apply

- ❓ *Think about your past in terms of what you have been worshipping and how you have been obeying God. How does it humble you?*

- ❓ *Since you came under Christ's rule, how have you changed? How do you need to go on changing?*

Rebellion reversed

Read Ezekiel 20:30-44

Idolatry leads to horrific outworkings (v 30-31). It's worth remembering that we are easily able to see the vile outworkings of idolatry in other societies; less so in our own culture and hearts. Children still suffer as parents serve the gods of career, immorality, leisure, comfort, and so on.

- ❓ *What do the people want (v 32)? Will they have it (v 33)?*
- ❓ *What will they get instead (v 34-38)?*

God's grace to his people is that they are not allowed to do, or to have, what they want! They can serve idols (v 39); but God will rescue them from their own folly (v 40-42).

- ❓ *What is the response of people who have been saved from their idolatry (v 43-44)?*

⌃ Pray

It's not popular or easy; but verse 43 is worth applying to ourselves as we speak to God. And it enables us to use verse 44 to thank God for saving us—giving us not what we deserve, but what he has promised. He is an amazing God!

Bible in a year: Exodus 11 • Psalm 78 • Colossians 1 • Revelation 1

It will come

Some truths are hard to bear. But that doesn't stop them being true…

Read Ezekiel 20:45 – 21:32

Judgment encompasses

❷ *What was Ezekiel to preach, and to which areas?*

- *20:45-48* • *21:2-5* • *21:28*

❷ *How were his words received (20:49)?*

Remember the context: Ezekiel is speaking to those already in exile about the coming fall of Jerusalem. It would have been more comforting to dismiss his words as mere stories—but it did not stop them being true. Judgment was coming, whether or not they accepted it.

☑ Apply

We live in a world which is facing a coming judgment. God has told us it will come; but most people dismiss it.

❷ *Do you truly believe judgment will come?*

❷ *How, and why, are you tempted to dismiss judgment as a "parable"?*

❷ *What difference will judgment make to how you live and speak today?*

Ezekiel 21:18-23 pictures the king of Babylon deciding who to attack: the Ammonites, or Jerusalem? The Ammonites were terrorists (Amos 1:13–14) and insulted Jerusalem in its fall (Ezekiel 21:28). But the answer from the casting of lots will come: destroy Jerusalem (Ezekiel 21:22).

Judgment destroys

❷ *How is the sword of judgment described (21:9-11, 14-17)?*

God's judgment is terrible, and it is just. Israel had violently rebelled against God, allied with his enemies, and mistreated the innocent among them (20:31).

☑ Apply

❷ *What would it look like for God to repay you for how you've treated him, and treated others?*

❷ *When we say, "Jesus has taken our judgment", this is what he has taken. How does this move you to praise, adore and worship him?*

There is hope

Read Ezekiel 21:25-27

Ezekiel points forward to the hope of a future king. The monarchy of Judah will be ruined (v 26); but it will also one day be restored (v 27). This king will be lowly in the world's eyes, but exalted by God (v 26).

☑ Apply

That same King taught his followers that they, too, should be low in the world's sight, and exalted by God (Matthew 20:25-28). What would this kind of spiritual humility look like in your life?

Bible in a year: Exodus 12 • Matthew 26 • Mark 14 • 1 Corinthians 5

Whose side is God on?

Nations and leaders have often used religion to validate their own political claims. But it is quite clear here whose side God really is on...

... and it's nothing to do with race or with nationality!

Two ways to live

Read Psalm 1:6

❓ *What is the contrast made in verse 6?*

❓ *What do you think it means for the Lord to watch over us?*

It is significant that the verse uses the personal name of God, Yahweh (usually written as LORD in our English translations). Those who reject God will ultimately wither and die. Those who love him are watched over by the God who has saved us and has committed himself to us in the promise of the gospel. **Read Hebrews 13:5.**

There are millions of choices before us. What to wear; who to support; what job to do; where to live; who to marry; how to spend our money; which friends to cultivate; what books to read. But there are only two ways to live. And we express which way we have chosen to live in the way we make each and all of these decisions in everyday life.

The God who watches

"God is watching you—from a distance" goes the song. But nothing could be further from the truth. This verse reveals to us that God is watching us in an intimate, detailed, caring way that is filled with love. It's a closeness that those who don't know him feel uncomfortable with. But those who have experienced his saving love welcome it, revel in it and rejoice about it.

If you never got round to memorising Psalm 1, why not have a go this week? Then you can sing it to yourself all day, every day.

⌄ Apply

❓ *How do you react to the thought of God's constant watching presence?*

❓ *When something in the next week goes wrong for you, how can you use this truth to calm and encourage yourself?*

❓ *What would you have thought or done differently last week if you'd really known God was watching?*

❓ *What will you do differently this week because you remember he is watching?*

⌃ Pray

Read through this psalm once again. Let its view of life challenge yours. Let its concerns become yours. Let its promises be yours to hold on to.

Then pray through each verse, pausing to thank God for what you find there, and/or to ask God to help you live according to the truths you see.

I won't tolerate it

We live in an age of tolerance. To be labelled "intolerant" is a real insult. And so our default position is: it's not our place to judge. But might it be?

Wicked tolerance

Read Ezekiel 22:1-16, 26-28

Israel wrongly tolerated injustice, false worship, immorality and wicked leadership.

- ❷ *Pick out both what the injustice was, and who got hurt, in: v 4, v 6-7, v 9, v 12-13.*
- ❷ *Pick out what was false about the worship in: v 4, v 8, v 9, v 12.*
- ❷ *What was wicked about their leaders, and specifically their spiritual leaders (v 6, 26-28)?*

God cares about how he is worshipped. And Israel's priests had forgotten that. They profaned what God called sacred and holy.

···· TIME OUT ···

Israel failed to value life as God did. Israel opted to worship created things instead of God.

- ❷ *In what ways does your society do the same?*

··

All of Israel's wickedness is a consequence of one thing: "You have forgotten me"(v 12). It's good to remember that sin is primarily a wilful forgetfulness of who God is.

- ❷ *What question does God repeat in v 2? What is the "right answer"?*

"Tolerance" can become a god. We worship it, trust it to right all that is wrong, and sacrifice justice, truth and God's standards at its altar.

Righteous intolerance

Read Ezekiel 22:17-29

- ❷ *What is going to happen to this society that tolerates sin (v 17-22)?*
- ❷ *What is God intolerant about (v 23-29)?*

☑ Apply

In verse 2, God calls Ezekiel to share his intolerance. In fact, all God's people are to do this (1 Corinthians 2:15-16).

- ❷ *Are there things—perhaps widely accepted by your society (or even your church)—which you need to be more intolerant of?*

Stand in the gap

Read Ezekiel 22:30-31

God looks for just one man who will stand before him and plead for the people, as Moses had (Exodus 32:30-32). "I found no one" (Ezekiel 22:30)—and so judgment would come. Thank him for now having provided that man in his Son, who gave his life so that he could stand before his Father on our behalf, that we need not be destroyed. **Read 1 Timothy 2:5-6.**

Another tricky chapter

Remember that God is the husband of his people—and so to love and worship anything other than him is spiritual adultery.

These are God's words, and they are here for a purpose. So take a deep breath and...

Read Ezekiel 23:1-49

The two kingdoms of God's people are represented here as Oholah (Samaria, i.e. the northern kingdom) and Oholibah (Jerusalem, i.e. the southern kingdom). The "adultery" that God has in view here is the two kingdoms' constant desire to trust alliances with other nations to protect them from trouble, and rescue them when they were in trouble.

Began in disgrace

Both these women "were mine" (v 4). In Egypt and as they entered the promised land, God's people had in fact been one nation/woman, both loved, called, rescued and blessed by him.

❓ *What became of Oholah (v 5-10)?*

···· TIME OUT ···

❓ *What does this imagery teach us about:*
  • *what sin is?*
  • *what worshipping false gods does to us?*

Continued in lewdness

Oholibah (the southern kingdom) saw what happened in 722 BC, when the northern kingdom was invaded and destroyed by the Assyrians they'd sought alliance with.

❓ *How did Oholibah respond (v 11-21)?*

Verses 36-39 outline in gruesome detail what this actually looked like in reality.

Oholibah was not content to "love" the Assyrians; she "slept with" Babylon, too.

❓ *What is pictured in verses 40-41?*

⌄ Apply

❓ *What are the "loves of your life" that provoke you to be unfaithful to God?*

Ended in ruin

❓ *What does God promise to do (v 22-27)?*
❓ *How is this pictured in verses 32-34?*

This chapter uses strong and startling language. Perhaps God needs to be so forceful in order to enable his people then, and his people today, to begin to grasp the horrific nature of their sin. We are naturally spiritually adulterous, too: we are overly impressed with the things of the world, and love them too much. We should drink "the cup of ruin and desolation", too. Yet this is the cup Jesus took for us (if you have time, read Luke 22:41-44). It is worth meditating on this: when we say "Jesus took my place and bore my sin", the Ezekiel 23 women depict who he "became"; our adultery is what he bore. Thank him now.

MARK: Introducing the Son of God

A symphonic opening

Read Mark 1:1-8

❷ *What does Mark want us to know as he starts his book (v 1)?*

❷ *What else do we hear about Jesus' identity?*

These verses are like the opening of a symphony, sounding the theme that the rest of the musical score will develop and explore. Who is Jesus? We hear an answer from Mark himself (v 1), from the prophets (v 2-3) and from John the Baptist (v 7-8). Mark is getting right to the point: this Gospel is going to be a stunningly compelling portrait of Jesus.

⌃ Pray

At the start of this series in Mark, pause to think about how well you know Jesus. What words would you use to describe him? In what ways do you wish you knew him better? Ask for God's help in seeing Jesus clearly as you read this Gospel.

A mixed quotation

Read Exodus 23:20; Malachi 3:1-2; Isaiah 40:3

❷ *Mark 1:2-3 is a mixed quotation from these three passages. Which portion comes from which Old Testament text?*

Exodus 23:20 is speaking about the people's arrival in the promised land. God promised to send a messenger ahead of his people. By applying this to Jesus, Mark is suggesting that Jesus brings deliverance, just like in the exodus. Meanwhile, Malachi 3:1 and Isaiah 40:3 speak of preparation for the coming of God.

❷ *In Malachi 3, what is scary about the Lord's coming?*

❷ *How does this help us understand John's message of repentance (Mark 1:4)? What is the danger if you are not prepared for God's coming?*

The testimony of John

❷ *What did John promise about the one who was coming (v 7-8)?*

The distinguishing mark of John's ministry is his connection to water, which symbolises cleansing from sin. But the defining mark of Jesus' ministry will be his connection to the Holy Spirit (v 8). Who could command the Spirit? Jesus must be God incarnate!

⌄ Apply

❷ *Imagine you were living in 1st-century Israel and hadn't heard of Jesus before. If you read the first eight verses of Mark's Gospel, what feeling would you be left with?*

❷ *How can you retain or rekindle a sense of awe at who Jesus is?*

The testimony of God

Mark has already told us in several different ways that Jesus is the Son of God—but now we're about to hear it from the Father himself.

Read Mark 1:9-11

❷ *Think back to the feeling you were left with at the end of the last study. How do these verses continue and/or contrast with what came before?*

We've already heard that the divine Son has come into the world. But the response of the Father is unique. Jesus is his beloved Son. The Father's words do not make that relationship; they highlight the loving relationship that has always existed.

There are many details in these few verses which demand an examination.

All heaven breaks loose

One surprising aspect of the story is the word Mark chooses for what happens to the heavens. Matthew and Luke say that the heavens were opened, but Mark says they were "torn open" (v 10). This fulfils Isaiah's prayer: "Oh, that you would rend [or tear] the heavens and come down" (Isaiah 64:1). The heavens are torn, and God comes to us.

Why does Mark specify that the Spirit descends "like a dove" (Mark 1:10)? I think it's to convey that this is not a swooping attack but a gentle hovering. The same Spirit once hovered over the waters at the beginning of time (Genesis 1:2). Now Jesus is bringing a new creation.

Read Psalm 2; Isaiah 42:1; Genesis 22:1-2

In Mark 1:11, the Father uses the language of Psalm 2:7 (about God's Son) and Isaiah 42:1 (about God's servant). So we are seeing two aspects of Jesus' identity. The divine Son has come to be the suffering servant.

❷ *What does Isaiah 42:1 tell us about what Jesus will do?*

❷ *What is the verbal connection between Mark 1:11 and Genesis 22:2?*

❷ *Why is the story of Abraham and Isaac significant for understanding who Jesus is and why he came (scan-read Genesis 22:1-14 if you need to!)?*

The people were to respond to the coming of the Lord with repentance. But there is a wonderful twist. As John preached repentance, Jesus identified himself with sinners through baptism. The divine Son came to be a sacrifice for sinners. He brought justice because he took the punishment for our sin and so restores us to relationship with the Father.

⌃ Pray

When we repent and believe that Jesus is the Son of God, and when we receive the benefit of what he has done, our testimony about the Son becomes similar to the Father's. The Father delights in the Son, and everyone who believes does the same.

Spend some time delighting in Jesus now. Tell him how much you love him and praise him for what he has done.

Bible in a year: Exodus 18 – 20 • Deuteronomy 5

News of the King

The next verses of Mark continue to set the stage for Jesus' ministry.

Read Mark 1:12-13

The Lord is my refuge

Just like Israel after their escape from Egypt, Jesus is led into the wilderness to face temptation.

Read Psalm 91:9-14

Why does Mark mention angels and wild animals? It's an echo of Psalm 91—the only place in the Old Testament that brings angels and wild animals together in regard to times of distress!

❷ *Scan-read Psalm 91. What light does Psalm 91 shed on how Jesus overcame temptation?*

The loving relationship between the Father and Son on display earlier (Mark 1:10-11) is still on display here. That relationship cannot be broken by anything! It is crucial to everything Jesus does. This sets the stage for the opening of Jesus' ministry.

Read Mark 1:14-20

❷ *What is Jesus' core message (v 15)?*

What is "the kingdom of God"? We might instinctively think of a place. But the Bible presents the kingdom not as a place but as a climactic event when God intervenes in human affairs. Jesus is the herald of this event. When he calls people to repent and believe, he is asking them to recognise their own rebellion against God and to accept

Jesus as their King. We see this in practice in the next verses.

The call

The simplicity of the formula "follow me" plus "[they] followed" (v 17-18) shows the reader the sheer power of the Creator at work. In the creation narrative, God said, "'Let there be light,' and there was light" (Genesis 1:3). It is a word of command, not a word of appeal. "One begins to see that becoming a disciple of Jesus is more of a gift than an achievement" (Christopher Marshall, *Faith As a Theme*, p 136).

The text highlights what these new disciples leave behind (Mark 1:18, 20). This is not a light thing to do! Following Jesus as Lord means relinquishing every worldly claim. It should radically impact how we relate to everything—family, job, money, food, and anything else we call "ours". Jesus is King of it all.

⌄ Apply

❷ *What temptations are you struggling with at the moment?*

❷ *How can you put Psalm 91:9-10 into practice?*

❷ *How does the notion of Jesus as your King help you and motivate you?*

Someone with authority

What do you think of when you hear the word "authority"?

In Jewish tradition, scribes taught by quoting other rabbis in a rapid-fire way—*Rabbi Hillel says... but Rabbi Gamaliel says... but Rabbi Eleazar says...* and so on. They were seen as authoritative in society—but their authority was always derived from someone else. Jesus' authority is different.

Read Mark 1:21-28

❓ *How do verses 23-26 demonstrate Jesus' authority?*

The demon's attempt to identify Jesus (v 24) is a hostile yet feeble attempt to confront the Lord of glory, who has all authority. It should probably be read as a naming ritual—an attempt to get control of the situation as well as power over the person by using their correct name. But the demon is powerless before the command of the Creator.

❓ *How do people respond (v 22, 27-28)? Do they realise who Jesus is?*

Read Mark 1:29-34

In Jesus' day, people did not have medicine to keep a fever from rising, and so fever was a deadly killer. The Old Testament sometimes presents fever as a divine punishment (Leviticus 26:16; Deuteronomy 28:22), and the rabbis regarded fever as a heavenly fire that only God could put out. So the healing of this fever is yet another proof of Jesus' deity.

We know news is spreading about Jesus, and in Mark 1:32 crowds begin to gather.

❓ *What do you think people are saying?*

❓ *Do you think they have grasped Jesus' core message (v 15)?*

Read Mark 1:35-39

❓ *What do Simon and the others seem to want Jesus to do?*

❓ *But what do Jesus' priorities seem to be in these verses?*

The whole city is at the door. Surely it would be a mistake to move on and not make the most of this moment. But Jesus' response shows that his top priority is not healing people or gaining fame. First he slips away to spend time alone with his Father. Then he tells the disciples that he has come to preach. The disciples and the crowds don't understand their main need: salvation. Healing and casting out demons are signs of the kingdom, serving to confirm the message that the King has come.

Pray

Spend some time praying for God's kingdom to come in the world around you. Pray for missions and the spread of the good news about Jesus; pray for those you know who need healing and deliverance; pray that your church community would be one that demonstrates the power, authority and salvation plan of the King.

Kiss the King

Rebellion against God's king is madness. It will only lead to destruction. Instead everyone needs to serve, celebrate and embrace the king. But who is this king?

Read Psalm 2

Revolution

King David is on his throne—he is the anointed one of verse 2 (see Acts 4:25). David's kingdom was enormous, and included other nations who should have been delighted to be under the care of the one true God and his king, David.

> ❷ *What did the nations and their leaders think of David's rule?*
>
> ❷ *How do people reject God's rule today?*

The Father speaks

In a remarkable few verses, each person of the Trinity speaks to reinforce David's astonishment. First the Father confirms the futility of rebellion; he "laughs", "scoffs", "rebukes" and "terrifies". It's sobering to think that rebellion is laughable and attracts the settled wrath of God. Why? Because of what God has already done—he has "installed" his king; and this king now speaks.

The Son speaks

The Lord's decree—his firm word—is now recounted by the son. It is a decree of absolute rule with no room for rebellion. For David, these words apply to his reign. However, the New Testament takes these verses and applies them again and again to King Jesus.

··· TIME OUT ································

Check out some of the New Testament quotes of Psalm 2: **Acts 4:25-26; Acts 13:33 and Hebrews 1:5.**

The Spirit speaks

Acts 4:25 tells us that the Spirit inspired David to tell everybody how to respond to the Father's son—the king. People must serve, celebrate and kiss him (i.e. acknowledge the king's right to rule them). This was a message about Israel's king, and, supremely, about King Jesus.

☑ Apply

> ❷ *What makes it hard for you to celebrate the King's rule? How does this psalm help?*
>
> ❷ *What will it mean to let King Jesus rule over everything in your life?*

The rule of David is seen in the reign of King Jesus—and that's a reign every believer will share. The words of Psalm 2:8 are applied in Revelation 2:26 to the church.

⌃ Pray

Confess areas where you reject the King's rule and ask the Spirit to help you serve, celebrate and kiss the Son. Rejoice that one day this is a rule that you will share with him into all eternity.

A wrench in the gut

We're in the final part of Mark's opening snapshot of Jesus' ministry in Galilee.

Read Mark 1:40-45

Willing compassion

In Jesus' times, few people were seen as more repulsive than those suffering from leprosy. This skin condition was a social death sentence. By Jesus' day, the rabbis had specified that those with leprosy had to remain 100 cubits (about 150 feet) away from others if they were upwind. If you came into contact with someone with leprosy, you would be declared unclean and would have to go through an elaborate cleansing ritual.

But the man in these verses dares to come close to Jesus.

> ❓ *How does the man demonstrate his faith (v 40)?*
> ❓ *How much does Jesus seem to be worried about becoming "unclean" (v 41)?*

Jesus is moved with pity or compassion (v 41). This is the wonderful Greek word *splanchnizomai*, which comes from a word meaning "guts". The man with leprosy would have turned the stomachs of others with disgust, but he turned the stomach of Jesus with love. Jesus is compassionate to the core. This compassionate heart is what Jesus reveals first, before he reveals his unparalleled power. Jesus doesn't need to touch the man to heal him, but he does.

> ❓ *What's the result (v 42)? What does Jesus tell him to do and not to do (v 44)?*

Once again Jesus shows his compassion for the man. The man would need the consecration of the priests to be reinstated into society. Jesus did not want him to remain in social isolation.

Unwanted fame

Jesus commands silence to prevent precisely what happens in verse 45. Because the healed man spreads the news, Jesus is in such demand that he cannot openly enter a town. People are desperate to see and hear him.

⌄ Apply

> ❓ *What circumstances might make someone an outsider or an outcast in today's society, and specifically in your own community?*
> ❓ *Who do you know who needs compassion?*
> ❓ *What could you do to help and love such people this week?*

⌃ Pray

It has been said, "All we need to bring to Jesus is our need".

> ❓ *How do you respond to this? How is it borne out by today's passage?*

Bring your needs to Jesus now.

Through the roof

The next section of Mark features a series of five controversies. Here's the first.

Read Mark 2:1-12

❓ *What's the setting (v 1-2)? What is Jesus doing?*

❓ *Who are we suddenly introduced to in verse 3?*

A typical house in 1st-century Israel had a flat roof. Sticks were laid on top of parallel timbers, a layer of reeds and branches was added, and the whole thing was over-laid with packed-down dirt. These men "unroofed the roof" (a literal translation) and dug an opening. Can you imagine the scene? Everyone in the house would hear the digging and tearing. Debris would fall. In today's society this would be a lawsuit waiting to happen!

❓ *But what does Mark tell us Jesus sees (v 5)?*

❓ *How does Jesus respond to this?*

Blasphemy?

The irony is thick in verse 7. Here is the teachers' logic: *We know God alone can forgive sins. Jesus claims to forgive sins. Therefore, Jesus is making himself out to be God. This is blasphemy.* Their question ("Who can forgive sins but God alone?") is right, but their conclusion ("He's blaspheming") is wrong.

❓ *How does Jesus prove he is God in verse 8?*

"Which is easier?" asks Jesus. Not which is easier to *do* (forgive or heal), but which is easier to *say*? Forgiveness is easier to claim because it is impossible to see from the outside. But physical healing is visible and external. It would be immediately evident to everyone if Jesus' word of healing failed.

❓ *How does Jesus prove that he is God in verses 10-12?*

··· **TIME OUT** ·····

Verse 10 is the first time in Mark that Jesus uses the title "Son of Man". This comes from Daniel 7.

Read Daniel 7:13-14

❓ *How does this help us understand where Jesus' authority comes from and what kind of authority it is?*

The miracles confirm the message: *Your God has come!* And this story demonstrates that Jesus did not come merely to show the power of God but to bring the salvation of God. The man left carrying his bed, but he no longer carried the burden of his sins on his back.

⌄ Apply

First, we should be like the paralysed man and accept that we need forgiveness and adoption into God's family more than anything else—and that both come through faith. Second, be like the friends and do your best to bring people to Jesus.

❓ *Who will you seek to speak to about the Lord Jesus this week?*

The call of Jesus

Of everyone you know, who might be least likely to come to Christ? Let your assumption be challenged today.

There's an important distinction in Mark between the crowds and the disciples. Both hear the teaching of Jesus, but only disciples follow Jesus. What accounts for the difference? The call of Christ. Jesus teaches the crowds, but he calls his disciples. Mark does not present any other psychological or situational indicator of why disciples follow Jesus. Jesus just says, "Follow me", and they follow. Mark wants the reader to see that becoming a disciple is a gift of grace.

Read Mark 2:13-17

❷ *Who else follows Jesus, apart from Levi (v 15)?*

❷ *How do the Pharisees react to this?*

Tax collectors were seen as traitors—they worked with the Roman oppressors. So, it was bad enough to call one tax collector to follow you, but to the Pharisees this looked like a moral pandemic! So many sinners gathering in one place—it could only be seen as a wicked feast.

In truth, though, this feast is a celebration of salvation.

Doctor Jesus

❷ *Who does Jesus compare these sinners to?*

❷ *What does that indicate about their future?*

The Pharisees see the tax collectors and sinners as hopelessly lost. But Jesus knows they are spiritually sick. He is not going to catch their contagion; he is going to heal it.

When Jesus says, "I have not come to call the righteous, but sinners", he is certainly not claiming that some people are righteous on their own and do not need a Saviour. He is taking the Pharisees' categories and turning them against them. The irony is that they need a doctor just as much as the tax collectors.

A seismic shift has taken place. The Messiah has come. He preaches the need to repent and believe the gospel (1:15). Those who reject his preaching, like the scribes, are actually on the outside of the kingdom, while those who receive it enter the kingdom.

⌄ Apply

We have sometimes reversed this in the history of the church. The respectable religious elite are often the most comfortable in church. The down-and-out can often feel the most uncomfortable in church. The church of Jesus should herald the heart of Jesus longing to receive sinners into his family. Those who come to him he will not cast out (John 6:37).

❷ *Who might feel uncomfortable coming to your church?*

❷ *What can you personally do to welcome sinners and outcasts?*

❷ *How can you pray for the leadership of your church about this?*

Bible in a year: Romans 8 • 1 Corinthians 13 • Ephesians 3 • 1 John 4

Weddings and wineskins

Following traditions can be comforting, stabilising and helpful—but we need to be careful…

Read Mark 2:18-22

❓ *What's the challenge brought to Jesus in verse 18?*

Jesus could have brought up the fact that the prescribed fasts of the Pharisees went beyond the Bible. He could have challenged the hypocrisy behind their fasting (as he does in Matthew 6:16-18). For the Pharisees, fasting had become a religious performance—something to show they were really serious about their religious practices. Jesus could have criticized this. But he chose to go to something much bigger.

❓ *Why don't wedding guests fast (Mark 2:19)?*

❓ *Who is the bridegroom in Jesus' analogy (v 19-20)?*

Jesus is saying that the people have the question all wrong because their entire orientation is off. They are asking how Jesus relates to fasting when they should be asking how fasting relates to Jesus. While Jesus is there, why would his disciples fast? It's a time for feasting!

Old and new

Jesus then uses two more analogies—both contain a contrast between the old and new and a warning not to mix them together.

❓ *What happens in each analogy when you mix old and new (v 21-22)?*

The teaching and practices of the Pharisees and scribes represent the old traditions. They have added many things to the Bible. These man-made rules and man-made traditions have become stiff and brittle. Jesus cannot be added to their traditions; he is like new wine that will bust their traditions wide open.

☑ Apply

What does all this mean for our own practices of fasting and other religious activity? It means that it needs to be oriented around Jesus, not our own traditions. Fasting, prayer, and obedience cannot make us acceptable to God or earn his favour. Of course, we can honour Christ with these things—for example, when we fast from things that get in the way of our relationship with him. But we should also celebrate Jesus. Joy is an essential part of Christianity, because the bridegroom has come! If any of our religious practices get in the way of our joy in Christ, we've gone wrong.

☑ Pray

Spend some time reflecting on what you've read. Ask God to show you how to apply this passage to your own life. Maybe you need help to take greater joy in Christ. Maybe there is something in your life you need to fast from to help you orient yourself around Jesus.

Bible in a year: Exodus 30 • Psalm 26, Psalm 43, Psalm 84

The wrong kind of rest

What do you think of when you hear the word "rest"? Do you ever try so hard to rest that it becomes more like work and stops being restful at all?!

Read Mark 2:23-28

The disciples are taking advantage of a provision in Old Testament law that allowed you to pluck ears of corn in another person's field (Deuteronomy 23:25). Yet the Pharisees challenge this as a scandalous breach of the law. The disciples haven't worked to produce the grain, but the Pharisees interpret even plucking heads of grain as work—which is forbidden on the Sabbath.

> ❷ *Is what the disciples are doing really unlawful?*

But Jesus doesn't use this line of argument. Instead he goes elsewhere in the Old Testament.

> ❷ *Was what David did lawful (Mark 2:25-26)?*
> ❷ *Why was it ok (v 27)?*

Jesus' situation has much in common with David's. In both cases, something unlawful happens that is not judged by God as a sin. In both cases, the leader's God-given authority enables the companions to eat something technically unlawful.

The Pharisees are making two errors. First, the Sabbath was made to serve humanity, not the other way round. It is supposed to be a pointer to Jesus' greater provision of rest, whereas the Pharisees see it as a work that earns God's favour. Second and more importantly, the Pharisees misunderstand

who Jesus is. Jesus is Lord; everything revolves around him.

The withered hand

Read Mark 3:1-6

> ❷ *What is the right answer to Jesus' question in verse 4?*
> ❷ *How does this challenge the Pharisees' understanding of the Sabbath?*

Jesus exposes the Pharisees' true motives. They have turned the Sabbath into a competition to see who can be best at doing nothing. But the Sabbath should be connected to God's heart to love and bless his people.

> ❷ *How does Mark describe the Pharisees' hearts (v 5)?*
> ❷ *How do verses 5-6 illustrate the contrast Jesus makes in verse 4?*

⌄ Apply

Reflect on the healing, life, restoration and rest that Jesus offers. Jesus' work is finished and we now rest in him—we don't need to earn God's favour. Spend some time celebrating that in whatever way is restful for you. You could listen to worship music or draw a picture that celebrates what Jesus has done and all that he has given you. Ask God to help you enjoy all his good gifts.

> ❷ *How does thinking this through either liberate you or challenge you (or both!)?*

Outsiders and insiders

What makes someone an outsider or an insider in God's kingdom? The next section of Mark zeroes in on that theme.

Read Mark 3:7-12

❓ *Why do so many people seem to be coming to Jesus (v 7-10)?*

Mark presents Jesus' encounters with demons as no contest. The demons immediately fall down before him and confess his identity. But Jesus doesn't want the demons to proclaim his name—he does not want to be seen to be in league with them.

True discipleship

❓ *What do you think it takes to be a disciple of Jesus?*

❓ *How might that be similar to the response the crowds make? How would it be different?*

❓ *How would it be similar and different to the response the demons make?*

Read Mark 3:13-19

The deeper work of cultivating disciples stands out as Jesus' special focus. The crowds learn about the gospel by hearing Jesus; the disciples learn to live the gospel by living with Jesus.

⌄ Apply

Sometimes it is easy to forget that we have a similar opportunity. Jesus promised he would be with us always, even to the end of the age (Matthew 28:20). Jesus is with us, and we must learn to cultivate our fellowship with him.

❓ *What distractions cause you to put Jesus off or displace him from the place of pre-eminence in your life?*

❓ *What is one way in which you can seek to "be with" Jesus (Mark 3:14)?*

Jesus' desire

The call to commune with Jesus can be heard as a burden. But Scripture confronts this self-centred focus.

❓ *How is it decided who gets to become a disciple (v 13)?*

Jesus desired us before we desired him.

Practical discipleship

❓ *The disciples don't just spend time with Jesus—what else do they do (v 14-15)?*

The disciples are apprentices, with Jesus' authority. They are now called "apostles"—which means "sent ones". Following Jesus means doing as he does.

⌄ Apply

Read Matthew 28:18-20

This is Jesus' commission to us all as his disciples.

❓ *What is one way in which you can put it into practice this week?*

Bible in a year: Jeremiah 17 • Ezekiel 20 • Luke 6, Luke 13

Sleep well

Those who trust King Jesus have confidence of final deliverance and eternal blessing.

Read Psalm 3

This short psalm is made up of three little sections, all of which conclude with the Hebrew word selah (end v 2, 4, 8). Each tells us something of the mind of King David as he fled Jerusalem from his son Absalom, who had rebelled against his father.

Many foes

Verses 1 and 2 of the psalm give us a vivid picture of just what David is up against. It's not just Absalom. Each of the three sentences begins with the same word: "many". David is really up against it. Nor are these just silent foes. They are rising up against him and spreading rumours that he is not God's anointed king (v 2).

❓ *How would most people respond to such danger?*

···· TIME OUT ··

To understand what David is facing...

Read 2 Samuel 15 – 16

Confident assurance

❓ *How does David respond (Psalm 3:3-4)?*

We might expect panic or desperation—after all, this is a king on the run for his life. But no—David still believes the promises of God and that God surrounds him with glorious protection. David's enemies may cause him to bow his head in shame, but his glorious God lifts his head up.

Assured deliverance

Having expressed this assurance, David can now get a good night's sleep. Verses 5 and 6 are remarkable, as anybody who is facing uncertainty can testify. It is David's knowledge of the character of God that allows him to rest, despite the desperate situation he finds himself in. His prayer (v 7) is a covenant prayer asking God to do what he has promised and make his enemies literally toothless. As this prayer is answered, David knows that he will again experience the covenant blessings of the Lord.

This prayer was also prayed by another King in David's line. His enemies were also many. Many scoffed as he hung upon the cross. But he entrusted himself to his Father's care, confidently knowing that he would be delivered from death. Christians can share David's confidence because King Jesus has prayed this prayer.

⌃ Pray

Re-read the whole psalm and use it to pray. Whatever dangers you face, you can be confident in God's final deliverance and blessing. Your enemies have been put under Jesus' feet and so you can sleep, confident in his sovereign rule over your life.

The family sandwich

No, not that kind of sandwich…

A sandwich is a literary technique in which an author begins and ends with one story, but something else is sandwiched in between. The middle story helps interpret the beginning and end.

Read Mark 3:20-35

- ❓ *Who does this passage start and end with?*
- ❓ *How would you summarise what happens in the middle?*

Demon-possessed?

The central section of the sandwich is verses 22-30. The teachers of the law cannot deny that the work of Jesus is supernatural, and there can only be two supernatural sources: God or Satan. So they say the work of Jesus comes from Satan.

- ❓ *What's the problem with the teachers' logic (v 23-25)?*
- ❓ *The strong man in verse 27 represents Satan. How does this image explain what Jesus is doing and how?*

Grave implications

The teachers have said that the work of the Spirit is actually the work of Satan. This is not a momentary mistake but an eternal sin—a blasphemy against the Holy Spirit. There is a fork in the road here. Someone is blaspheming—either Jesus or the Jewish leaders. Which side will the reader take?

--- TIME OUT ---
People with a tender conscience often ask if they have committed the unforgivable sin. But their sensitivity to repentance means they can't have committed it! The eternal sin is perpetual unbelief: saying that Jesus is evil. In that state, forgiveness can never come, because forgiveness is only found by embracing Jesus as the Son of God.

- ❓ *What is the encouragement in verse 28 to those who are worried about their sin?*

The bread

Jesus' family think they have a claim on him and want to take control of him—that's the subtext in verses 21 and 31-32.

- ❓ *Compare verse 21 with verse 22. What are Jesus' family members in danger of?*

Jesus says that those who sit at his feet are his true family (v 34). Why? Because they see that Jesus has a claim on them, not the other way round.

⌄ Apply

- ❓ *How might people act like Jesus' mother and brothers today?*
- ❓ *Why is that dangerous?*
- ❓ *What will it look like for you to pursue humility at the feet of Jesus?*

Bible in a year: Exodus 32 – 34 • 2 Corinthians 3

Whoever has ears

The parable of the sower may sound familiar and even cute—but it contains some serious and unsettling truths.

Read Mark 4:1-12

❓ *How does Mark set the scene (v 1)?*

A parable is a type of teaching a bit like a riddle. Some inside knowledge is required to crack the code that the parable uses.

Insiders and outsiders

❓ *What's the scene-shift in verse 10? Who is Jesus with now?*

❓ *What's the distinction Jesus makes in verse 11?*

❓ *How does that reflect the distinction between the crowds and the disciples?*

Jesus is about to give the disciples the inside knowledge they need to crack the parable.

Seed and the sower

Read Mark 4:13-20

❓ *What does the seed in the parable signify?*

❓ *Who is the farmer?*

❓ *Look back through what we've read of Mark so far and think about the people we've met. Which of them do you think corresponds to each type of soil?*

A change of heart

The parables are like a metal detector. It lets out a sound when it passes over metal. The parables are a heart detector. They pass over those with hard, shallow, or crowded hearts and there is no sound. But when an insider hears the parable, it makes an impact in their heart. Jesus preaches parables to bring this unseen division into the light.

❓ *How do you get to be an insider (v 11)?*

Deaf and mute

❓ *What is the effect of parables on those who don't have inside knowledge (v 12)?*

Why would Jesus not want people to turn and be forgiven? The context of his quote in Isaiah helps us. In Isaiah 44:18-20 we see that people become as deaf and mute as the idols they worship (see also Psalm 115:4-8). God turns such people over to judgment.

The right response to Jesus' words is not resignation or fatalism. The good news of the gospel goes out into all the world—and the Lord opens people's hearts to receive it. So we pray that he will soften hearts and open eyes around us as we share the gospel, and that he will bring a harvest that is thirty, sixty, or a hundred times what was sown.

☑ Apply

If you are a Christian, God has given you "ears to hear" (Mark 4:9).

❓ *How will you use your heart, your ears that hear, and your eyes that see today?*

Expectations shattered

When I was about 13, my brother and I played a game with glass bottles. We'd throw them in the air and hit them with a baseball bat to make an amazing explosion.

Jesus' parables are similar. He takes contemporary expectations of what the kingdom will look like, throws them up in the air, and shatters them with his verbal bat.

Read Mark 4:21-34

The lamp in verse 21 represents Jesus.

> ❓ *How have you seen people effectively try to "hide" Jesus?*

The preaching of Jesus exposes what is hidden in darkness, and it will also reveal the children of light—the ones who have ears that hear (v 23).

The flip side of the command in verse 23 is the warning in verses 24-25. If someone listens well and receives the truth, they will receive even more. If someone listens poorly, even the little they have understood will be taken from them.

The growing seed

> ❓ *What is Jesus' point in verses 26-29?*
> ❓ *The growing seed is like the growth of God's kingdom. So, why is this parable a challenge to those who think the kingdom will come as a result of their hard work of obedience to God?*

A small beginning

> ❓ *Why might it be surprising or challenging to think of the kingdom of God as a mustard seed (v 31)?*

> ❓ *In what ways did Jesus' first coming have a "small" or unimpressive appearance?*
> ❓ *But what does this parable suggest about its future?*

Jesus' teaching has sometimes been called "the already / not yet". The kingdom has already come, but it is not yet here in its fullness. One day Jesus will come again, and it will be big and obvious and overpowering.

Mark concludes with a return to the insider/outsider theme. Once again we hear that the crowd only receive parables, while the disciples privately receive more revelation and explanation (v 33-34).

Jesus shares big truths about the kingdom, which the disciples need to grow into. The parables test our spiritual appetites: do we want to learn and grow? Do we have shallow or crowded hearts like the soils in the parable of the sower, or will we ask Jesus questions and dig into his word?

☑ Apply

> ❓ *How well are you listening to God's word (v 24)?*
> ❓ *In what ways do you need God's help to grow and bear fruit?*
> ❓ *What have you understood about God's kingdom that you want to thank him for? What are you still finding confusing?*

Lift up these things to God now in prayer.

Bible in a year: Exodus 38 – 40 • Psalm 27

What no one else does

We now begin a long section of signs and responses. Jesus' signs prove his identity, but only some can see it.

The first boat miracle

There's a rhythm in the next four chapters of Mark with bread miracles for the crowds (6:30-44; 8:1-10) and boat miracles for the disciples (4:35-41; 6:45-51), culminating in a scene that involves both bread and a boat (8:10-21). Today we'll look at the first boat miracle: the calming of the storm.

Read Mark 4:35-41

Notice the physical reality of the storm (v 36-37). Try to imagine what it was like!

❷ *What is Jesus doing (v 38)?*

The way the disciples frame their question in verse 38 is important, and not well translated in most English Bible versions. They frame it in a positive way: "You do care that we are perishing, don't you?" The disciples do believe that Jesus cares, but their trust is disrupted by the storm.

Suffering disrupts our trust too. We think God cares, but when suffering comes, it can seem as if he is sleeping. In the boat, Jesus actually was sleeping!

❷ *How does Jesus' sleep show us that he is human?*

❷ *How does Jesus' sleep demonstrate his faith in God?*

Be still!

Read Psalm 107:28-30

❷ *Who is it who calms the storm here?*

❷ *So what does Mark 4:39 tell us about Jesus?*

Jesus' calm sleep suggests that he has great trust in the Father who can control the storm; but Jesus is not just an example of faith—he is the object of faith. He has no need to cry out to God to still the storm. He stills it himself.

The disciples should be glad like the sailors in Psalm 107:30 because their lives have been spared. Why are they more afraid now than when they thought they were going to perish? Fear is a frequent response to a supernatural sign in Mark. Jesus has just shattered their pre-existing categories. The disciples think Jesus is the Messiah. But they begin to wonder if he is more. Are they meeting their Maker in that boat?

⌄ Apply

It's easy to spiritualise this story and make it all about Jesus stilling our storms of suffering today. But this passage is first and foremost about Jesus. We need to see what it says about him before we see what it has to say about us.

❷ *What have you learned about Jesus in this passage?*

❷ *How can these things help you when you face scary situations?*

My name is Legion

Jesus now leaves Jewish territory and enters the region of the Gerasenes.

Read Mark 5:1-20

A man in the tombs

In verses 2-5 Mark emphasises the impurity of the man: he has an unclean spirit and he lives in an unclean place (the tombs). He also emphasises the fact that no one can subdue him, and that he is tormented.

> ❷ *In the light of those things, why is what happens in verses 6-8 so surprising?*

Jesus makes the demon tell him its name (v 9). A legion was the largest unit of troops in the Roman army—about 5,600 soldiers. This man has an entire army of demons living in him and tormenting him. But they are no match for the almighty army of one.

> ❷ *What happens next (v 11-13)?*

An angry mob

The herdsmen flee and the townspeople come to see what has happened.

> ❷ *What do they see (v 15)?*
> ❷ *How might you expect them to respond?*
> ❷ *Why do you think they are afraid?*

The crowd begs Jesus to go away (v 17). They would rather have an army of evil spirits in their region than the Saviour of the world. Being without Jesus would be better than being with him.

> ❷ *But how does the man respond differently (v 18)?*

> ❷ *What mission does Jesus give him, and what's the effect (v 19-20)?*

Jesus is the stronger one who plunders Satan's kingdom (3:27). But he is a surprising Messiah. The Jews expected a second exodus redemption in which the Messiah would destroy their enemies. The first exodus had seen the Egyptian army drown in the sea. This time Israel assumed the Roman army would meet the same sort of fate. How surprising to see an army of demons drown in the sea instead.

···· TIME OUT ·····································

Isaiah has something to say about this man.

Read Isaiah 65:1-5

> ❷ *What are the connections between this passage and the demon-possessed man?*

Remember that this story takes place in Gentile territory, in the region of the Gerasenes (Mark 5:1). This story is a fulfilment of Isaiah 65:1. Jesus is revealing himself to a nation that has not called on his name.

⌄ Apply

> ❷ *What do you have in common with the demon-possessed man? What has Jesus done for you?*
> ❷ *Who will you tell about it?*

Bible in a year: Leviticus 4 – 6 • Psalm 20

The daughter sandwich

None of us want to feel broken—but sometimes it's actually a blessing.

Read Mark 5:21-43

❓ *Who is Jairus (v 22)?*

❓ *What kind of attitude does he seem to have to Jesus (v 23)?*

❓ *What does he ask Jesus to do?*

Jairus does the same thing as the demon-possessed man in the previous story—both "beg earnestly" (v 10, 23). In the original language, the wording is the same.

"Little" is a term of endearment—like when I call one of my teenage daughters "baby girl". We learn later that she's twelve years old (v 42). This girl is desperately ill, but Jairus believes that Jesus can make her live (v 23). We start to sense where the story's going—until we're suddenly interrupted.

Another daughter

❓ *What do we learn about the suffering of the woman in the crowd (v 25-26)?*

A woman was considered unclean during her menstrual cycle. But this woman's blood flows continuously, not just once a month. Not only is she sick, not only is she unclean all the time, she's also run out of money. Again, she's like the demon-possessed man: no one can help her (v 3-4, 26).

❓ *What does she believe about Jesus (v 28)?*

❓ *What does that lead her to do?*

Jesus knows the woman needs more than healing. So despite the disciples' rebuke, he keeps looking around (v 30-32). Finally the woman cannot stay hidden. Like Jairus, she falls at his feet.

Why does Jesus draw her out? He knows that this woman needs her shame to be broken. She needs to be set free in front of everyone. Jesus also knows that the woman needs a family. So he calls her "daughter". We started the story with a request to heal Jairus' daughter—but Jesus is saying, *I've got to stop for a moment and heal and restore my daughter.* She hasn't just been healed; she's been made his child.

Little girl

❓ *What's the result of Jesus' delay (v 35)?*

❓ *How does Jesus respond in verses 36-39?*

Honey, time to wake up, is what Jesus is saying in verse 41 as he pulls the girl out of death. He acts like a true parent, making sure she gets something to eat (v 43). Jesus cares for every detail of this girl's life—just like he did for the woman in the crowd.

⌃ Pray

It's easy to pretend to be strong and self-sufficient, but to know Jesus' tenderness and power we need to rely on him and not ourselves. We need to come to him with our brokenness and seek his help.

❓ *How will you do that right now?*

Peace in trouble

Though David, the anointed king, feels surrounded, he still experiences deep and lasting peace. And so can we.

Read Psalm 4

❓ *What evidence do you see (e.g. repeated words) that this psalm is closely linked to Psalm 3?*

Enemies (again)

Psalm 4 echoes much of the previous psalm and is probably from the same time in David's life. He is still beset by enemies and cries out to his "righteous God" for help (v 1). The phrase "give me relief" literally means "enlarge my narrow places"—in other words, David feels cornered.

❓ *What situations in life make you feel trapped like David?*

Who's cornered?

These enemies have robbed the king of his glory (v 2) and are pursuing lies (an alternative way to translate "false gods"). But the last laugh is with David. To all intents and purposes he may appear to be the one who is trapped, but in fact it is his enemies who are truly cornered. Verse 3 explains why. David is the anointed king whom God has set apart, and God will surely hear his prayer.

This is a complete turnaround, as David makes clear in verses 4-5. Rather than David shaking with fear, it is his enemies who should be trembling. David preaches to them: *Don't sin! Search your hearts! Be silent! Trust God!*

The promise still holds

Of course, it does not seem that way to outsiders. No wonder they are asking questions (v 6). But the original promise of Numbers 6:25, which is repeated in the second half of Psalm 4:6, is still true. And therefore David can pray for joy and express a deep and lasting peace. Despite all evidence to the contrary, he is not cornered.

⌄ Apply

This is another song sung by our King, Jesus. His own people, the Jews, sought delusions and lies and turned his glory to shame—or so they thought. And yet the Father did shine his face upon him. Jesus rose from the grave to bring peace and security to every believer.

❓ *Look back at the situations you listed earlier. How do the death and resurrection of Jesus change how you think about these?*

⌃ Pray

Thank God that he set apart his faithful servant, Jesus. And thank God that he hears his Son's prayers for his people. Pray for the joy and peace that result.

Homecoming?

The contrast between the stories of faith in Mark 5 and the story of unbelief that begins Mark 6 could not be more tragic.

Read Mark 6:1-6

Jesus leaves the Sea of Galilee and travels 25 miles southwest to his hometown of Nazareth. He goes to the synagogue and begins to teach.

In Luke's Gospel, when Jesus teaches at the synagogue in Nazareth, he turns to a text in Isaiah 61 about the coming of the Messiah. He says, "Today this scripture is fulfilled in your hearing" (Luke 4:21). We don't know whether this was the same occasion as that in Mark 6 or a different one but, either way, the inhabitants of Nazareth would have heard Jesus' claim to be the Messiah.

❷ *What's the initial response to Jesus' teaching (v 2)?*

❷ *But how does it turn sour (v 3)? Why do they take offence?*

Two natures

"Where did this man get these things?" (v 2). He did not get them from his earthly family. It sounds like the sort of thing you'd say if someone from your hometown became a famous actor. But the Nazarenes aren't proud of Jesus. They think they know him because they know his occupation and his family, and so they cannot accept that he's something special. This is why the proverb Jesus quotes in verse 4 is true.

Mark's Gospel presents two images of the Son. Sometimes we see the "royal" image

(Jesus' glorious divine identity), and at other times we see the "servant" image (his humble earthly origins). But we don't have to choose between them. Jesus is both. That is what people repeatedly fail to understand.

▼ Apply

❷ *In what situations might you forget or doubt that Jesus is really God (with all God's power)?*

❷ *In what situations might you need to remember that Jesus is human (and gave up so much for us)?*

Unbelief

The wording of verse 5 can make it seem like Jesus is limited and powerless un-less people have faith—like in the movie *Elf*, where Santa's sleigh can't fly without Christmas cheer. But that's not the case. Throughout Mark, people come to Jesus because they believe he can heal. Unbelief would prevent them from coming.

❷ *Why is their unbelief so amazing (v 6; look back at verse 2)?*

▲ Pray

❷ *Is there anything holding you back from putting your faith in Jesus at the moment? What doubts do you have?*

❷ *Will you bring these things to him now in prayer?*

Bible in a year: Leviticus 9 – 11 • Psalm 23

A dangerous mission

Today's passage is another sandwich.

Jesus sends out the twelve disciples in 6:7-13, and they return in verse 30. What happens in the middle? The beheading of John the Baptist (v 14-29). The middle of the sandwich foreshadows the rejection that Jesus and his messengers will receive.

Read Mark 6:7-30

❓ *What does Jesus send the disciples to do (v 7, 12-13)?*

❓ *How do we see a sense of urgency in verses 8-11?*

Jesus tells the disciples to take the same things God commanded the Israelites to bring in their flight from Egypt (Exodus 12:11). There is an overtone of judgment here—but this time judgment will fall not on the Egyptians but upon all who don't repent. Shaking the dust off your feet (Mark 6:11) is something Jews would do when they left Gentile territory. It's communicating that this place is not part of God's people.

The unbelief of Herod

Now for the middle of the sandwich.

❓ *What are people saying about Jesus (v 14-15)? What does Herod think?*

❓ *Why had John the Baptist been killed (v 17-28)? What had John done and who had nursed a grudge against him (v 18-19)?*

❓ *What did Herod think about John (v 20)?*

Herod (or Herod Antipas) had persuaded his half-brother's wife to divorce her husband and marry him. John courageously declared that this was against Jewish law. Herod thought highly of John, but he feared man more than God and loved sin too much to let go and repent.

▼ Apply

John the Baptist had been preaching the same message of repentance as the disciples. It was not received well. We should not be naïve about the cost of discipleship and the fact that repentance is not a popular message. Yet in verse 30 we see the disciples coming back on a high. There have been ministry successes to celebrate. We shouldn't be naïve—but we also shouldn't be defeatist. The gospel is wonderful, and powerful to overcome opposition.

❓ *How does this challenge or alter your own view of discipleship and mission?*

An amazing difference

Both John and Jesus were killed by political tyrants who vacillated but in the end feared other men too much. Both were righteous, innocent victims. But there is one amazing difference. John died because of the sin of others; Jesus died for the sins of others. Repentance matters because it brings hope of forgiveness. But there is no saving sacrifice for those who deny they are sinners.

The first bread miracle

We're in the middle of a pattern of public bread miracles and private boat miracles. The first bread miracle might be Jesus' best-known miracle of all.

Read Mark 6:31-44

❷ *In verses 31-32, where do Jesus and the disciples go and why?*

❷ *How would you expect them to feel when they see the crowds (v 33)?*

❷ *But how does Jesus feel (v 34)?*

"The LORD is my shepherd; I lack nothing" (Psalm 23:1). This passage is the fulfilment of that ancient hope. Here is good news for those who know they are harassed and helpless. Jesus is the long-awaited Shepherd, who satisfies his sheep, providing both spiritual and physical food.

❷ *What problem arises and why (Mark 6:35-36)?*

❷ *What seems to be wrong with Jesus' proposed solution (v 37-38)?*

Yet in the end all the people eat and are satisfied. Mark also tells us that there were twelve baskets of food left over. Each of the twelve disciples had his own basket of leftovers as a physical reminder—a faith souvenir to mark this moment.

Biblical echoes

Jesus is like Moses, providing bread from heaven (see Exodus 16). He's like Elisha, who saw more than enough food miraculously provided in 2 Kings 4:42-44. He's the Shepherd of Psalm 23, who leads his people to green grass and gives them what

they need. He's the fulfilment of Ezekiel 34, where the prophet highlighted the problem of a lack of good shepherds for the "flock" of God's people (v 1-6), and promised that God himself would come to be their Shepherd (v 11-16).

The feeding of the 5,000 isn't just an isolated event, an impressive miracle or a practical solution. Once again, it's a demonstration of who Jesus is.

❷ *Why do you think it matters that Jesus is following biblical patterns and fulfilling Old Testament prophecies?*

❷ *What are we learning about who Jesus is and what he's like?*

The good Shepherd

Read Ezekiel 34:11-16

❷ *What does God promise to do for his "sheep"? This is in picture language, but what do you think it means that God would do literally?*

❷ *How are these things true of Jesus?*

As Christians today, we are part of the flock of God's people. What God says in this passage is a description of the way he treats us, not just the way he promised to treat Israel or the way Jesus treated people in his own time.

❷ *What does this passage lead you to want to pray today?*

Another boat miracle

I wonder how easily you forget that Jesus is with you—and what happens when you do.

Read Mark 6:45-52

❓ What makes the disciples and Jesus separate in verses 45-46?

❓ In verse 47, where are they all?

❓ What are the disciples experiencing (v 48)?

The word "straining" suggests a tormenting kind of pain; it's used elsewhere for the torment that comes from demon possession (Mark 5:7), childbirth (Revelation 12:2) and even hell (Revelation 14:10). The disciples are separated from Jesus, and it's not going well!

But there is hope. Mark does not simply tell us what is happening with the disciples. He explicitly tells us that Jesus sees it—and he does not turn a blind eye.

❓ How does Jesus go to them (Mark 6:48)?

Passing by

What in the world does it mean that Jesus "was about to pass by"? (The ESV actually says, "He *meant* to pass by them".) Is Jesus playing games? No. This is a fulfilment of the Old Testament.

Read Exodus 33:19 and 1 Kings 19:11

❓ Who "passes by" in these verses?

❓ So what does this suggest about who Jesus is?

I AM

❓ How do the disciples react when they see Jesus (Mark 6:49-50)?

Most translations obscure the meaning of Jesus' response in verse 50. He says, "*Ego eimi*"—which can indeed mean "It is I". But it can also mean "I AM"—the divine name. Once again, this is exactly what God did for Moses (Exodus 34:5-7). He declares his name. Jesus is saying, *Do not fear, because I am God!*

❓ What do you think of the disciples' response (Mark 6:51-52)?

🔽 Apply

The Bible is the place where we most often encounter God today. So, think: when you read the Bible, are you ready to see God? It's easy for our reading to become just a cerebral exercise. But God is the divine author, and he intends to reveal himself. We should not respond with hard hearts.

Pray now that God would reveal himself to you, then re-read today's passage and respond to it.

You are what you eat?

What makes you holy or unholy, clean or unclean? What you wear? What you eat? Or something else?

Read Mark 6:53 – 7:16

Jesus is performing many healings (6:53-56), but the religious authorities ignore that in this fresh confrontation.

❓ *What do they focus on (7:5)?*

❓ *What's the background to this (v 1-4)?*

This was not just a hygiene issue; it was a question of ritual purity. This tradition, although not part of the Old Testament law as such, had become so intertwined with Jewish religion that people believed that to be Jewish was to wash hands, cups and vessels before eating.

Mark specifically mentions the fact that they would wash after coming from the marketplace (v 4)—which is where Jesus has just been performing miracles (6:56). So the Pharisees and scribes believe that Jesus and his disciples are acting in an unclean way.

❓ *Why does Jesus call the religious teachers hypocrites (7:6-8)?*

❓ *What's wrong with holding onto their human traditions (v 8-9)?*

"Corban" involves saying that your money or possessions are devoted to God and therefore can't be used for anything else. But this is leading the religious elite to break the fifth commandment and fail to care for their parents (Exodus 20:12). They invoke God's name to avoid doing something which God himself commanded.

What's inside?

❓ *What do you think Jesus might mean in Mark 7:15? What won't the religious teachers allow to "go into" them? What "comes out" of them?*

Read Mark 7:17-23

❓ *Why are the religious teachers' traditions misguided (v 18-19)?*

❓ *What really makes you unclean (v 20-21)?*

Holiness is a matter of the heart, not the hands or the stomach. Jesus refers to the heart three times (v 6, 19, 21). The Pharisees think the disciples' hands are defiled, but Jesus gives them an x-ray that shows them that they are hypocrites with defiled hearts. Their insides are rotten.

⌃ Pray

Re-read the list in verses 21-22 and ask God to give you an x-ray of your own heart. Are any of these things coming out of your heart? Praise Jesus for offering true purity, confess your sin and ask for his help to change. Then ask him to forgive you.

You might find it helpful to pray while washing, as a physical reminder that Jesus has done all that is necessary to cleanse you.

Crumbs from the table

Mark 7 has raised the issue of whether hands or foods can be unclean. But underneath there is a much uglier question. Can there be unclean people?

Read Mark 7:24-30

Tyre was a Gentile region at least 20 miles from Capernaum. Jesus has entered a house and is trying to keep his presence quiet (v 24). But he can't remain hidden.

> ❷ *Who comes to fall at his feet (v 25-26)? What does Mark tell us about her?*

This woman is a definite outsider. Even Jewish women did not approach Jewish rabbis. And Gentiles were not supposed to do so either—certainly not a Gentile woman who had a daughter with an unclean spirit! This woman has three strikes against her.

But...

"She begged Jesus" could be translated as "She kept begging Jesus" (v 26). This woman is gutsy, despite the unpromising situation.

Jesus' response seems offensive at first glance (v 27). It looks like a racial insult. The Jewish people are the children. The Gentiles are the dogs. But this is not an insult. It is a parable. He is imagining a family meal. Jesus uses a form of the word for dogs which means "puppies". These are beloved pets. They will be fed. But they are not fed first. There is an order to Jesus' mission— the Jews first, and then the Gentiles.

> ❷ *Is the woman offended (v 28)?*

Stop the music. This woman is the first example in Mark of someone who actually understands a parable and responds rightly. No one else has really understood Jesus' mission. She understands it after hearing one sentence in the form of a parable. And she not only understands it—she does not argue against it. She enters the world of the parable and refuses to leave. She reasons from within the world of the parable and finds hope there.

> ❷ *What hope does she see (v 28)?*

True cleanness

In Jesus' time, this Gentile woman would have been regarded as an unclean dog. Yet this story turns the tables on all that. The inside makes someone clean. And this woman is clean because she is full of faith.

⌄ Apply

The woman does not hear the answer she wants in verse 27. But she accepts what Jesus has said and still finds hope in who he is.

> ❷ *When have you found that God has not given you the answer you want, or the thing you want, or the circumstances you want?*

> ❷ *What would it look like for you to say, "Yes, Lord" and ask for his help, like the Gentile woman?*

The morning after

Our Christian faith allows us to be confident in all circumstances.

Read Psalm 5

❓ *How would you sum up David's attitude towards his enemies?*

Things always look different in the morning. This psalm probably continues from the previous two. If so, there has been a remarkable turnaround in his thinking. Previously, he was overwhelmed with the number of his enemies (Psalm 3:1). Now, he is confident that they will not be able to stand before his "King" and "God".

A confident plea

David's prayer is one of confidence. Yes, he asks to be heard (Psalm 5:2). But within the space of a few lines, he expresses an assurance that God will hear him (v 3). What has made the difference? It is nothing less than the character of God.

---- TIME OUT ----------------------------------

❓ *What is it about God's character that should make us confident about our prayers?*

....

David's confidence is more than an assurance of answered prayer. He is also confident in the Lord's justice over his enemies (v 4-6). The language is strong: God cannot abide wickedness. That's why David is sure that he will make it back to the temple (v 7).

A realistic plea

The morning allows David to see things more clearly. His enemies have not disappeared—and so he needs to make two requests of his God. First, he needs to ask God not to let him follow the same paths (v 8). Second, he needs to ask God to deal with his enemies appropriately (v 9-10).

A public plea

In the last part of the psalm, David is praying in public. He is encouraging the Lord's people to share his confidence tinged with realism. He needs to encourage his people to find both their joy and protection in their God.

This song of confidence and realism has been sung by a greater anointed King: Jesus. God has delivered him from his enemies and now he leads us, his spiritual choir, in the same refrain.

▾ Apply

Reflect on situations where Christians need to share both the confidence and realism of this psalm.

❓ *How do these two need to be held together in your own life, with its particular challenges?*

Be opened!

What would you say if someone asked you what Jesus is really like?

Read Mark 7:31-37

Jesus' journey in verse 31 is not a direct route but more of a semi-circle. It's a 120-mile journey! He seems to be deliberately staying in Gentile territory.

❓ *Who does Jesus meet there (v 32)?*

Jesus takes him aside from the crowd privately. The scene is so personal. But what Jesus does is also perplexing. Why does he put his fingers into the man's ears and touch the man's tongue (v 33)? Jesus can just say the word and the man will be healed! Here is the glorious, wonderful answer: Jesus is using sign language. He is taking the time to use touch to explain what he is going to do.

He looks up to heaven (v 34)—always seeking the Father and doing what the Father would have him do. Before he speaks, he sighs. Jesus feels this man's pain before he brings the healing and the joy.

Literally, verse 35 says "the chain of his tongue was broken". The chain that has kept him in the bondage of silence is broken. Jesus came to bring liberty for every kind of captive.

❓ *How do people respond (v 36-37)?*

Re-creation

The form of "he has done everything well" in verse 37 is closely linked to the Greek text of Genesis 1:31: "God saw all that he had made, and it was very good". God created a world with no deafness or muteness—until sin entered in. Now the Creator has stepped onto the stage of the world he created. Wherever he goes, he is undoing the effects of the fall and bringing a new creation.

❓ *Do you think the people in the Decapolis understand this?*

A portrait

This passage is a beautiful portrait of what Jesus is like. He's the Creator of the world, with all power; he's the Son of God, who defers to his Father; he's the breaker of bonds and the freer of captives; he's full of compassion and tender care.

🔽 Apply

Think of one person you'd like to share the gospel with, or maybe someone with whom you've already had one or two conversations about faith. Which of the aspects of who Jesus is do you think they don't know? How could you tell them? Spend some time thinking about how your conversation could go.

Then spend some time praying for them—and praying for an opportunity to make that conversation happen.

Bread and boats

We're at the end of the first half of this Gospel. Mark ties things together in a masterful way.

Read Mark 8:1-13

Four thousand

The bread miracle in verses 1-10 stresses the same points that the first bread miracle highlighted.

- ❓ *How do we see Jesus' heart of compassion?*
- ❓ *Why is the disciples' response disappointing (v 4-5)?*
- ❓ *What's the miracle and what's the result (v 6-8)?*

Once again we have a sign that Jesus is the Son of God—which is why it is so jarring to immediately overhear the Pharisees' demand for a sign (v 11).

- ❓ *What's the difference between Jesus' response to the crowds and his response to the Pharisees?*
- ❓ *What do you think causes this difference?*

Bread in the boat

Read Mark 8:14-21

Jesus warns the disciples of the yeast of the Pharisees and of Herod. This "yeast" is the response to Jesus of unbelief.

- ❓ *How did the Pharisees show unbelief just before this (v 11)?*
- ❓ *What did Herod's unbelief consist of (look back at 6:14)?*

❓ *What do the disciples think Jesus is talking about (8:16)?*

We have assumed so far that the disciples are insiders—they have eyes to see. Now Jesus' confrontation puts a question mark over that assumption. Why are they worried about having no bread? How can they still be so blind and deaf and hard after this string of signs he has given (v 17-21)?

It's easy to look at the disciples and feel smug. How could they keep forgetting the things that Jesus has done—first at the feeding of the 4,000, and now here in the boat? How can they not understand? But Jesus' questions in verses 17-18 can apply to us too. There are so many things we've seen Jesus do—in the Bible, and in our own lives. But what happens when the next hard thing comes? It's so easy to panic and say, "What are we going to do? How could this ever work out?" Our initial impulse is to doubt and not trust; to panic and not praise.

So the question this text has for us is the same one that Jesus had for his disciples. You have seen the signs. Do you understand?

⌃ Pray

Pray for your own heart, eyes and ears—and for the heart, eyes and ears of those you love. Ask Jesus to keep on teaching you about him and to help you trust in him.

RUTH: The sojourn

This is a story with a dark and difficult beginning. In the first five verses of the book of Ruth, things just go from bad to worse.

Read Ruth 1:1-5

This story took place during the time in which "the judges ruled" (v 1). This was a period of spiritual darkness, when God's people repeatedly rebelled against him and were punished. Ruth zooms in on one particular family's trials and tragedies.

Elimelek's family

❓ *Who are the key characters in these verses? Try drawing a family tree.*

❓ *What goes wrong for this family to begin with (v 1)?*

We should read this situation with Deuteronomy in mind. God promised blessing on his people for obedience (Deuteronomy 28:1-14), but curses for disobedience—including famine (28:15-68). During the time of Ruth, this warning came true. The fields were barren and the crops failed.

But instead of mourning over the sin of the land and asking God to restore things, Elimelek left the fields of Bethlehem for Moab. This move was not like that of a person today migrating to another country. God had promised that his presence would dwell in Israel. So by moving away, Elimelek was turning his back on the Lord.

⌄ Apply

Elimelek's name means "My God is King". He did not listen to his own name. He made his decision without reference to God.

❓ *What upcoming decisions do you have?*

❓ *How can you make sure you go God's way rather than your own way?*

From bad to worse

❓ *What else goes wrong for Elimelek's family (Ruth 1:3, 5)?*

❓ *How do you imagine Naomi felt by the end of verse 5?*

Naomi did not know how things would turn out, but readers have the privilege of knowing her whole story. It is a story that will go from emptiness to fullness, from tragedy to glory. It shows us that God is still trustworthy in the midst of emptiness and difficulty. The question for us is: can we bring ourselves to trust him when we suffer?

In these verses there is just a tiny hint at the future that God has prepared for Naomi. She comes from Bethlehem, which of course is associated with David and ultimately the birth of Jesus. It is actually from Naomi's insignificant family, in an insignificant little town, that the Saviour of the world, the King of kings, would come.

⌃ Pray

Spend some time praising God for the way that he works through all things—including disasters and darkness, and every apparently insignificant detail of our lives.

Road to return

Looking back over our lives, we can often see significant moments, where change occurs. What key turning points have you faced in your life?

In today's passage there is a geographical and a spiritual turning point. It is about turning back to Bethlehem, and also about turning back to the Lord in faith.

Read Ruth 1:6-10

Verse 6 contains many hints about the nature of the wonderful provision of our God. He allowed Naomi to *hear* the news from Israel; he came compassionately to *visit* those suffering in famine; he came to his people, with whom he had made a covenant; and he did not overlook their basic needs but gave them food. This was the context in which Naomi, Ruth and Orpah had to decide what to do next.

The decision

❓ *What does Naomi tell Ruth and Orpah to do?*

❓ *What is her hope for them?*

❓ *What is her view of God?*

The word "kindness" is the rich Hebrew word *hesed*, which refers to God's loyalty, faithfulness, grace, mercy and compassion. Naomi believes that God is indeed kind, and that his power and grace extend beyond the borders of Israel.

Naomi compares the way Ruth and Orpah have treated her with the way she hopes God may treat them (v 8). These daughters-in-law have been compassionate to Naomi, and so she longs for them to be richly blessed. Specifically, she prays for them to be settled and secure, and for the Lord to bless them both with another husband.

❓ *What words would you use to describe Ruth and Orpah's response (v 9-10)?*

⌃ Pray

❓ *Who do you know who reflects the kindness of God? Praise God for them and pray for them. Consider sending a message to thank them.*

❓ *Can you think of times when God has dealt kindly with you? Praise him for this.*

❓ *Do you ever find it hard to think of God as kind? Why? Ask him for his help with this.*

Your people

One theme in the Bible that is often overlooked, especially in individualistic cultures, is the concept of community. Yet it is a theme woven throughout the Bible. God displays his glory to and through his people: we are saved into a community.

Ruth and Orpah express a desire not only to go with their mother-in-law but to go to her people (v 10)—severing ties with the Moabites. This idea was extraordinary in the ancient world. It hints at the possibility of conversion. They have a chance to become part of God's people.

Bible in a year: Numbers 7 – 8 • Psalm 66, Psalm 99

Your God, my God

When did you first profess faith? What led you to that decision?

Today's passage gives us a portrait of a conversion—and of faith that's worth imitating.

Read Ruth 1:11-14

Naomi's opinion is firm. She advises her daughters-in-law to turn back.

It was customary for a childless widow to marry her husband's brother in order to raise children and continue the dead husband's line. But Naomi's two dead sons have no brothers, so there is no hope of that happening. Since her family line cannot continue, she wants Ruth and Orpah to remarry and start new families.

> ❓ *How does Naomi describe what has happened to her family (v 13)?*

> ❓ *Who does she see as the main victim?*

Naomi blames God and doesn't have much hope for the future. But she does at least see God's involvement in her life. She knows that things are not outside of God's sovereign control.

Orpah kisses her mother-in-law goodbye. But Ruth clings to her tightly.

Risk-taking faith

Read Ruth 1:15-18

Orpah's decision makes sense on a practical level, but Ruth's decision is based on active faith.

> ❓ *In what ways does Ruth express faith here?*

> ❓ *Who and what does she commit to?*

In Hebrew poetic structure, the sentence or word that comes in the middle is often the most important. Here, verses 16 and 17 frame Ruth's glorious profession of faith: "Your people shall be my people, and your God my God".

Ruth's declaration is not primarily about her commitment to Naomi. It is about her commitment to the Lord.

⌄ Apply

> ❓ *Do you think your faith is more like Naomi's or more like Ruth's? Or do you struggle to have faith at all?*

> ❓ *How could you show faith like Ruth's, practically speaking? You could ask someone to pray with you about this.*

⌃ Pray

Ruth had lived with Naomi for ten years. While Naomi does not appear to have been a winsome witness, it is clear that somewhere along the way Ruth heard of and believed in the God of Israel, by his grace.

We must pray that God would use us to lead more "Ruths" to faith. Pray that you may "be wise in the way you act towards outsiders," speaking winsome and gracious words, and that he would use you to bear witness (Colossians 4:2-6).

Bible in a year: Psalm 50 • Numbers 9 – 11

The arrival

Naomi has had some terrible losses—but also some very good news. Now she is back in Bethlehem where she started. How will she describe her journey so far?

Read Ruth 1:19-22

❓ *Why do you think the women say, "Can this be Naomi?" (v 19)?*

❓ *How does Naomi describe herself?*

Naomi means "pleasant" and Mara means "bitter". Naomi believes her situation demands a new name—one that reflects her frustration.

···· TIME OUT ····

The name "Mara" has a noteworthy history. When God's people rebelled in the wilderness, complaining about a lack of provision, Marah was the name of the place where they grumbled against him (Exodus 15:22-25). They could not drink the bitter water, so they cried out to the Lord and he made it drinkable and sweet. Naomi reflects the heart of her ancestors: she complains about her situation, failing to see the grace of God in her life (expressed in part by the daughter-in-law who stands beside her). We wonder if the bitter one will ever become sweet again.

Can I vent?

Naomi is having a venting session. Maybe it will help things! She attributes her pain to God; strikingly, there is no acknowledgment of personal accountability. She also forgets that it is part of God's character to care for widows (Exodus 22:22-23; Psalm 68:5; 146:9).

❓ *What four things does Naomi say the Lord has done to her?*

🔼 Pray

Do you know anyone who might describe their situation the way Naomi does? Psalm 146 talks about how God helps the oppressed and needy. Look it up and use it to help you to pray for them.

Another return

There are some similarities between Naomi's return and the story of the prodigal son (Luke 15:11-32). In rebellion, the son turns his back on his father and leaves for a far country, where he squanders his money. Then there is a famine and the son is so hungry that he longs to eat pig food. Eventually he wakes up to the reality that in his father's house there is "food to spare" (v 17)—and he returns.

Unlike the prodigal son, Naomi does not return broken and contrite. She expresses bitterness instead of brokenness. However, Naomi is also returning home at the prospect of bread. She comes back at the beginning of the barley harvest in Bethlehem—which literally means "house of bread". There is a new beginning agriculturally. Will there be a new beginning in other ways for these women—as there was for the prodigal son?

The Lord has heard

Even in the deepest troubles, we need to remember that God does not forget his promises.

❓ *How do discouraging situations affect you physically? And spiritually?*

Read Psalm 6

This psalm is sober, accompanied by the sad strings. No wonder, because David is in deep distress and feels the discipline of the Lord upon him (v 1-3). He recognises that even in his darkest moments God is teaching him something. That doesn't make the pain any easier, and it affects both his body (v 2) and his spirit (v 3). All he can do is cry out, "How long?"

···· TIME OUT ···

❓ *What changes in our perspective when we remember that God can and does teach us something during difficulties?*

David's plea

David's plea to the Lord (v 4-5) is instructive. He doesn't claim to be innocent; rather, he appeals to two things. First, he reminds the Lord of his covenant promises (v 4). Then, in a surprise twist, he tells God to keep him alive so he can praise him (v 5)! God deserves the king's praise, and it's only a living, breathing king who can sing the songs.

David's testimony

David is honest with God and now we return to the opening melody. The situation David is in has worn him out. The sorrow he feels keeps him awake at night and his eyes are so raw he can barely see. Many of us have had nights like this!

All change!

Then something miraculous happens! David's attitude completely turns around. His night of painful reflection pays dividends. As David has poured out his soul to God, he has come to realise what God knew all along—the covenant promises will never fail. David can therefore send his enemies away with a confident shout (v 8-10).

✔ Apply

As Christians, we do have nights like David's. Difficulties are part of the sovereign Lord working in our lives to teach us something. We need to understand that his word will not fail. How do we know? Not because of a promise made, but because of a promise fulfilled. The Saviour has come. God has rescued. So God will keep us until the end.

❓ *In which area of your life do you need to cling on to this? Or do you need to share it with a Christian friend to encourage them?*

⌃ Pray

Pray that you/your friend would cling on.

Introducing Boaz

Keep your eye on this guy! In Ruth 2 we meet a "worthy man"—someone of wealth and integrity.

Throughout the rest of the book we will see that Boaz is a model of integrity, compassion, and justice. But he is also a picture of Christ. Boaz's grace points to Jesus' grace—the grace that has bought our salvation, and the grace that strengthens and empowers us to love this broken world. Look carefully at the way Boaz treats Ruth, because it is also the way Jesus has treated us.

The field

Read Ruth 2:1-3

Boaz is a relative of Naomi's husband—"from the clan of Elimelek" (v 1, 3). This detail will become significant later!

> ❷ What is Ruth's hope as she goes out to glean?
> ❷ How does she end up in Boaz's field?

Gleaning consisted of gathering leftover grain. God's law commanded harvesters to leave the edges of the field for the poor and not retrieve dropped crops (Deuteronomy 24:19-22; Leviticus 19:9-10). This was a way to help the poor survive—though it still required effort and work on their part.

Ruth goes to the fields with a sense of humility. She recognises her need for favour. She illustrates the proverb "[God] mocks proud mockers but shows favour to the humble and oppressed" (Proverbs 3:34) and the words of James: "God opposes the proud but shows favour to the humble" (James 4:6).

Perfect timing

Read Ruth 2:4-7

The ESV says, "And behold, Boaz came from Bethlehem" (v 4). There is a note of wonder in the word "behold", preparing us to hear that Boaz has arrived—just at the right time.

> ❷ What is our first impression of Boaz (v 4)?
> ❷ What impression does he gain of Ruth (v 6-7)?

⌄ Apply

Ruth is dependent on others' favour, yet she does not wait around for help. She tries to make the very best of her situation that she can, working hard and trusting God to be good to her as she does so.

Meanwhile, Boaz's faith is expressed in an everyday greeting. He has the Lord on his mind in the ordinary routine of life.

> ❷ Is there anything that you are waiting for the Lord to do? Do you need to trust him more? Do you need to work hard and take steps yourself?
> ❷ How could you keep God in mind during your everyday life?
> ❷ How could you use your words to build up and bless others each day this week?

Bible in a year: Numbers 16 – 18 • Psalm 96

Faith and favour

Have you ever felt totally overwhelmed by someone else's kindness? That's how Ruth feels in today's passage.

Read Ruth 2:8-13

Boaz is determined to provide for Ruth. He does not only tell her that she may glean in his field but actually insists that she stay there (v 8-9).

> ❓ *How else does Boaz show favour to Ruth in verses 8-9?*
> ❓ *Why is Ruth so surprised at this (v 10)?*

In addition to food provision, Boaz goes on to show favour to Ruth in another way. He blesses her with his words. You can imagine what the affirmation of a godly, influential leader must have sounded like to her.

> ❓ *What does Boaz praise Ruth for (v 11)?*

Boaz believes that what Ruth has done is a result of her faith in God. It is the Lord whom she has pleased by her actions (v 12).

> ❓ *What image does Boaz use to describe Ruth's faith?*
> ❓ *Does this image feel like a good description of your own relationship with God? Why, or why not?*

···· TIME OUT ····································

The psalmists also use the image of wings to express trust in the Lord (Psalm 17:8; 36:7; 91:1-4). A similar image is used by Jesus when he weeps over Jerusalem, saying that he longs to gather them as "a hen gathers her brood under her wings" (Matthew 23:37). How sad it is that people reject Christ's salvation and his rest!

Pause now to thank God for his rescue and protection. You may want to ask him to make this sense of refuge and safety more real to you. Ask for his help in telling the world where to go to find this eternal grace.

Mercy and justice

> ❓ *How does Ruth summarise what Boaz has done for her (Ruth 2:13)?*

Boaz provides for the hungry—following God's word regarding the widow, the stranger, and the poor. He also protects Ruth, charging the men not to harm her. He uses his influence for those who have no influence. And he uses his words to bless Ruth, showing her personal dignity and respect.

Boaz exemplifies mercy, justice, and the grace and favour which God shows to his people. He is an example of Micah 6:8:

"And what does the LORD require of you? To act justly and to love mercy and to walk humbly with your God."

⌃ Pray

Pray for those in your community who are in need of provision, protection or dignity.

Pray for yourself and those who are close to you. Ask God to show you how to act justly, love mercy and walk humbly with him.

Roasted grain

We might like to think of today's passage as Boaz and Ruth's first date. But it is not a romantic evening meal—more like a lunch break at work.

Even so, Boaz's hospitality is gracious and exemplary.

Read Ruth 2:14-18

> ❷ *How does Boaz continue to welcome Ruth?*
>
> ❷ *How does he go above and beyond his duty?*

As a result of Boaz's kindness, Ruth gathers an abundance: a whole ephah of barley. That's some 13.6 kg (30 pounds) of food— several weeks' worth. Ruth apparently hauls this back to Naomi's place all by herself. This Moabite can carry some grain!

⌄ Apply

Ruth shows the same kindness to Naomi that Boaz has shown to her. Her example is challenging.

Do you find it hard to love bitter people and to serve difficult people? If so, then allow Ruth to instruct and inspire you! Love the "Naomis" in your life in the way that Christ has shown love to you.

> ❷ *Who do you find difficult to love?*
>
> ❷ *What could you do to love and serve them today?*

Hope for the future

Read Ruth 2:19-23

> ❷ *Who does Naomi bless (v 19, 20)? Why?*

Naomi seems to be saying that the Lord is showing kindness to her whole family—to her and to Ruth, both women with deceased husbands. But how can the Lord show kindness to the dead?

Boaz is a kinsman-redeemer (v 20). The law instructed that when a man died, his brother was obliged to marry his widow and raise his children. He was even to give the dead man's name to the first child born out of the new marriage. This would ensure that the inheritance would continue to be associated with the dead relative. If Boaz is willing to act as a redeemer for Naomi's family, he can marry Ruth and continue the family line of Elimelek.

> ❷ *What other reasons are there for Ruth to stay in Boaz's field (v 21-22)?*

Ruth and Naomi are vulnerable widows in a patriarchal society. They need provision now and security for the future. They cannot solve this problem on their own: they need a redeemer. A husband and a child for Ruth will end the crisis, provide for their needs, and continue the family line.

⌃ Pray

Think of anyone you know who seems to be in a hopeless situation. Pray that God will bless them. Thank God for the hope that he has given you for the future, and the eternal security that you have in Christ. Ask for strength to share this hope with others.

Bible in a year: Numbers 21 • 2 Kings 18 • John 3 • 1 Corinthians 10

At the threshing floor

Chapter 2 left us hanging. Will anything happen between Ruth and Boaz?

Naomi is determined to ensure something does happen between them.

The plan

Read Ruth 3:1-5

> ❓ *What is Naomi's hope for Ruth (v 1-2)?*
> ❓ *What are the steps of Naomi's plan?*

The threshing floor was the place where farmers would get rid of the chaff—the unwanted husk around the kernel of grain—by tossing the harvested grain into the air with a pitchfork. This was done at night because night breezes were needed to blow the chaff away. Naomi sees an opportunity for Ruth.

Ruth is to uncover Boaz's feet and lie down close to him. The purpose of such a sensual gesture is intended to communicate something to Boaz. Apparently it was a customary means of requesting marriage.

This is a risky plan. Boaz could respond harshly or accuse Ruth of acting like a prostitute. He could easily assault her if he wanted to. As Naomi gives these instructions and Ruth wholeheartedly accepts them, they are both displaying enormous trust in Boaz. The plan all depends upon his integrity.

Apply

The same is true for us as Christian believers. We can take risks for Jesus because we know we can depend on his kindness, integrity and redeeming power.

> ❓ *What risks are you afraid of taking for Christ? Write down something you will do this week to step out in faith.*

The proposal

Read Ruth 3:6-9

> ❓ *How is Boaz's shock and confusion communicated (v 8-9)?*
> ❓ *What does Ruth ask Boaz to do?*

"Spread your wings" (or "garment") is elsewhere an idiom for marriage (see Ezekiel 16:8). It is also the image Boaz used to describe how Ruth sought refuge in God (Ruth 2:12). Now Ruth is asking Boaz to become part of God's protection and provision for her life.

Boaz is "a redeemer", not "the redeemer". Naomi has other male relatives, so Boaz is not obliged to marry Ruth. But Ruth knows he is willing to follow the spirit of the law, not just its minimum requirements.

Pray

Reflect on Jesus' character and ask for his help in trusting him. Pray for friends who find it hard to trust Jesus. You could send them a message reminding them of his trustworthiness.

The answer

What will Boaz say? Will he marry Ruth?

Read Ruth 3:10-13

It turns out that Boaz is not put off by Ruth's directness but pleased by it.

❷ *What is his initial response (v 10)?*

It seems safe to assume that Ruth is younger than Boaz. She could have gone after young men (literally, "choice men"), but decided not to pursue a guy out of greed, nor out of passion. Instead she has other values, such as family loyalty.

Stepping back for a moment, we are left to marvel at the purity of both Boaz and Ruth. Instead of engaging in some steamy sexual encounter, Boaz praises God for Ruth! Nor does Ruth make any sexual advances towards Boaz in an effort to win him.

We can imagine how fast Ruth's heart must have been beating—but Boaz comforts her by saying, "don't be afraid" (v 11).

❷ *What does Boaz promise to do (v 13)?*
❷ *Why (v 11, 12)?*

Provision

Read Ruth 3:14-18

Before it is light enough for people to recognise Ruth, Boaz sends her home. This is meant to preserve her dignity and reputation.

❷ *How else does Boaz care for Ruth (v 15)?*

The gift of grain is not only a provision of food. It is a message to Naomi. Boaz is serious about his pursuit of Ruth—so serious that this will involve caring for her mother-in-law too.

Naomi once described herself as "empty" (1:21), but now she has a full load of grain before her. We are witnessing her journey from emptiness to fullness, through the actions of Ruth and Boaz.

⌄ Apply

How similar Boaz's treatment of Ruth is to the way the Lord Jesus has dealt with us! We can be like Ruth, going to him respectfully but boldly to ask him to spread his "wings" (2:12) over us and redeem us. He has made a promise that all who call on his name will become part of his bride, the church (Romans 10:9; Ephesians 5:28-33). And he has given us the most wonderful provision: the Holy Spirit who dwells in us. The Spirit is the "firstfruits" which promises more to come, assuring us of "the redemption of our bodies" (Romans 8:23).

❷ *What rescue or provision are you desperate for in your life or ministry?*
❷ *Are there things you particularly long for the Holy Spirit to do in and through you?*

Spend some time bringing these things to God, and praising him for his abundant and gracious provision.

Looking through Boaz

Before we reach the final chapter of Ruth, it is worth pausing to understand more about the concept of redemption in the Bible.

In Old Testament law, a redeemer was someone who protected and helped his relatives.

Read Leviticus 25:25-28, 47-49

- ❷ *Who or what can be "redeemed" in these verses?*
- ❷ *Why is redemption necessary?*
- ❷ *Who can be a redeemer?*
- ❷ *What is the result of redemption for the person who is being helped?*

The story of God's people also reveals the fact that God himself is a redeemer. In the exodus, the people of Israel were enslaved in Egypt. They were desperate and in great need. So God promised redemption.

Read Exodus 6:6-8

- ❷ *Why is redemption needed here?*
- ❷ *What will God do to redeem his people?*
- ❷ *What is the result of redemption for the Israelites?*

Our Redeemer

The New Testament is clear that all of us are spiritually helpless and in need of redemption. But God "has rescued us from the dominion of darkness and brought us into the kingdom of the Son he loves, in whom we have redemption, the forgiveness of sins" (Colossians 1:13-14).

Redemption always has a price. In the Old Testament laws, it happened through a commercial transaction: a kinsman had to make a payment to redeem property and slaves. In the exodus, the payment for deliverance from Egypt was the sacrifice of a precious lamb at Passover (Exodus 12).

Read Ephesians 2:12-13, 19-22

- ❷ *In what ways were we in the same position as Ruth (v 12)?*
- ❷ *But what price has been paid (v 13)?*
- ❷ *And what is the result?*

To be a redeemer you had to have both the willingness and the ability to redeem. Boaz had both. He demonstrated the character of a redeemer through his selfless actions, and his status as a landowner meant he had the financial capacity to become a redeemer.

Only Jesus had the immeasurable worth necessary to redeem sinners. And he was willing: he was full of kindness and grace. He has made us part of his family, just like Old Testament redeemers, and just like the Israelites in the time of the exodus.

When we look at Boaz, we see many godly traits to imitate. But when we look through Boaz, we see the gospel of Jesus Christ.

Pray

Psalm 107 contains more examples of redemption. Use this psalm to help you "ponder the loving deeds of the LORD" (v 43)—including the redemption you have in Christ.

Bible in a year: Numbers 26 – 27, Numbers 36 • 1 Chronicles 7

Search my heart

David's trouble, which we've seen him pouring out in the last few psalms, prompts some serious heart searching—which turns into a deep confidence in God.

❓ *What tends to be your immediate response to difficulty or danger?*

Read Psalm 7

David's search

We don't know all the precise details of the circumstances surrounding this psalm, but it's clear David's in danger. The language of verse 2 is pretty graphic! What's significant about this psalm is how these trials make David think. His first response is not to cry out for help (that will come later). His first response is to search his own heart (v 3-5).

···· TIME OUT ····

Our sins are paid for by Christ. We should not therefore think of God as treating us in a tit-for-tat way, but we do still need to share David's thinking. **Read Hebrews 12:4-12** for help with this.

David's vindication

Only in Psalm 7:6 does David turn to a familiar appeal for help. This is expressed in courtroom language. David is asking for God the Judge to prove David's right standing by judging his enemies.

❓ *Read Acts 17:31. When will we see God's final vindication?*

David's salvation

David is not just looking for a courtroom declaration. He needs and wants God to act. His appeal to God Most High (Psalm 7:10, 17) is a reminder to God of his promises from long ago—it is a description used at the time of Abraham (Genesis 14:18). God's faithfulness to his promises means deliverance for David, described in very physical and final language (Psalm 7:12-13). The funny thing is, God often does not need to intervene, because evildoers end up trapped by their own schemes (v 14-16).

❓ *In what ways do people's evil deeds catch up with them?*

▾ Apply

David's song (v 17) is one of exuberant praise—ours can be, too. God has vindicated his Son, who was surrounded by enemies, even death. All are now overcome.

❓ *What would it mean for you to praise in the middle of difficulties in your life?*

▲ Prayer

Take a moment to sing the praises of the Lord Most High, whatever circumstances you are in today.

Two redeemers

All eyes are on Boaz as he goes to make good his promise to Ruth.

There is another possible redeemer for Ruth and Naomi—a closer relative than Boaz. Boaz goes to find him.

At the city gate

Read Ruth 4:1-4

Legal transactions, judicial proceedings, and official business were all conducted at the city gate. It was also the best place to find someone: everyone in the city regularly passed through this gate. So Boaz sits here to wait for the other potential redeemer to come through.

> ❷ *How does he explain the situation to the other redeemer (v 3)?*
>
> ❷ *What next steps does he suggest (v 4)?*
>
> ❷ *How does the other redeemer respond?*

The land in question is all of Elimelek's property that had not been sold when the family made the journey to Moab (v 9). It was probably all that Naomi had. Presumably it was due to the desperate situation of herself and Ruth that Naomi needed to sell it.

Raising this issue of Naomi's property may be a way for Boaz to divert attention away from Ruth, in order to win her for himself. Or perhaps this is simply the most straightforward way of introducing the matter. Whichever, it is clear that redeeming Ruth and buying Naomi's land go together—as Boaz reveals next.

The true cost

Read Ruth 4:5-6

> ❷ *Why does the other redeemer change his mind?*

Redeeming the property would involve sacrifice. Redeeming Ruth by marriage as well as buying the field would require resolve and even the risk of losing a good reputation (since, as Boaz emphasises, Ruth is a Moabite).

This was not the only cost. When a widow was redeemed, the first son born in the new marriage would be recognised as the son of the woman's first husband, inheriting his property when he grew up and so perpetuating the name of the dead in his land (Deuteronomy 25:5). So if the other redeemer had a child with Ruth, he would eventually lose the field he had bought.

He is more concerned with his own welfare, property, and posterity than with the welfare of his relative, Naomi. By contrast, a true redeemer is willing to pay a price for the good of others.

⌂ Pray

Reflect on the cost of your own redemption. Spend some time praising God for Jesus.

What price may you need to pay to serve Christ and others? Pray that God will give you the willingness to do so.

Sealing the deal

The matter is settled. Boaz is the only one willing and able to pay the price.

Read Ruth 4:7-10

Boaz's "purchase" is confirmed through an ancient custom: removing a sandal.

With the official business complete, Boaz offers a speech—bookending it with the phrase "You are witnesses," just in case any future questions arise concerning the transaction.

But one more significant thing happens at the city gate.

A prayer of blessing

Read Ruth 4:11-12

- ❓ *What is the people's prayer for Ruth?*
- ❓ *What is their prayer for Boaz?*
- ❓ *What is their prayer for the family as a whole?*

Rachel and Leah were the wives of Jacob. Together with their two servants, Bilhah and Zilpah, they bore twelve sons whose descendants made up the twelve tribes of Israel (Genesis 29 – 30; 35:16-18). The people, then, are asking the Lord to give Ruth a place alongside these mothers of the people of God: that is, that she may be given a key role among God's people.

Tamar was the widow of Judah's son. She was childless, with no prospect of marrying again. So Tamar disguised herself as a prostitute, deceiving her own father-in-law, so that she might have a child by him (Genesis 38). Like Ruth, Tamar went out in active pursuit of a child and a better future.

Of course, Tamar and Judah's conduct was a lot less admirable than Ruth and Boaz's! But their union proved to play an important role in salvation history. God promised that the Messiah would come through Judah (Genesis 49:10), and Judah's strongest son was Perez, the son of Tamar.

The prayers of the people in Bethlehem were answered. Ruth did become a key person in the story of redemptive history. Boaz's family did have renown in Bethlehem. In fact, it was through Boaz's line that Israel's greatest king would come—King David (as we'll see at the end of the chapter).

⌃ Pray

You might not use the same examples as the people of Bethlehem, but it can be helpful to use Bible characters and Bible phrases to inform your prayers.

Choose a family you know. Consider the character traits of Ruth and Boaz—the way they are described and the way they act—and ask God to make the members of this family like that. Ask God to build his church through them and make them fruitful.

The end (almost)

The final section of Ruth reveals the staggering providence of God.

A son for Ruth and Boaz

Read Ruth 4:13

Saying that Boaz "took Ruth" is to say that he took her home—an expression for marriage. Adding "and she became his wife" seems redundant—it is saying the same thing a second time—but its inclusion emphasizes Ruth's new status. She has repeatedly been "the Moabite" and "the foreigner", lower than a servant (e.g. 2:10, 13). But here in chapter 4 she is Ruth, the wife of Boaz. She has a brand new status, thanks to the sovereign grace of God.

The two of them go from wedding to baby in one verse! Fertility has been an issue all the way through the story—both the infertility of the land and the problem of childlessness. Both these needs have now been met. The narrator only explicitly mentions the Lord's involvement twice: once regarding his provision of food (1:6) and now with his provision of a son (4:13).

A redeemer for Naomi

Read Ruth 4:14-17

- ❷ *What phrases do the women use to describe the child?*
- ❷ *Who else do they praise (v 14, 17)?*

Surprisingly, it is not Boaz who is called a redeemer here but his son. This child will bless Naomi personally and continue her

family line. How can we be sure of this? The women point to his mother: he will be like her.

Ruth's devotion to Naomi is so great that having her is better than having seven sons. Seven was a number of perfection and sons were highly prized; and it was the loss of her sons that was a key reason for Naomi's bitterness in chapter 1. This expression is the ultimate tribute to Ruth's amazing life and loyalty.

- ❷ *Compare this passage with 1:1-5. How have the calamities at the beginning of the book been solved?*
- ❷ *Compare this passage with 1:19-21. How has Naomi's personal situation been transformed?*

◢ Pray

- ❷ *In what ways has God worked throughout the story of Ruth?*
- ❷ *What surprises you about this?*
- ❷ *What comforts you?*

As you reflect on these things, spend some time worshipping God. Pray for anyone you know who is struggling at the moment—that they might know the extraordinary provision and care of the God who has redeemed them. Ask God to show you how he can use you, like Ruth, to bring fullness to those who are empty.

Good-news genealogy

Don't rush over the genealogy at the end of Ruth. It's a vital glimpse of the bigger story.

A king for Israel

Read Ruth 4:17-22

Ruth is not just a story about two desperate widows—it is also about a desperate nation "in the days when the judges ruled" (1:1). Israel was broken by immorality and disunity. Obed would be the grandfather of David, the king who would give God's people leadership, unity and security.

The ten names in 4:18-22 display God's answer to the prayer that Boaz and his line may be renowned in Bethlehem. Perez heads the royal line of Judah, which continues through a host of others to Boaz, Obed, Jesse, and finally David. The list is not exhaustive—there would have been other generations in between the names we read here (see 1 Chronicles 2). But it is meant to show the continuation of the line.

The future Messiah

David was Israel's most celebrated king. But more important than his military success was the promise that he was the paradigm for the future Messiah. God promised that one of David's sons would sit on the throne for ever (2 Samuel 7:12b-16; Psalm 132:12). This comes to fulfilment in Jesus.

Read Matthew 1:1-17

Matthew's genealogy shows that Jesus has always been part of God's plans. It also shows that Ruth's story is not unique—God

repeatedly incorporates unexpected and unworthy individuals into his people.

> ❷ *Pick out any names you recognise. What stories lie behind these names?*

Read Matthew 1:18-25

> ❷ *Look at how Jesus is described. In what ways is he like Obed, Boaz, and Ruth?*

> ❷ *In what ways is he better and greater than them?*

Think of the way in which Naomi and Ruth received provision from God. Were they just handed money? No! They experienced extraordinary kindness. The story ends with the picture of Naomi holding a child in her arms, having found real rest, peace and intimacy.

For Christians there is an even greater resolution. Jesus is "God with us". By placing our faith in him, we find ultimate refuge, ultimate rest and ultimate peace—in part now, and one day in full.

⌄ Apply

Reflect on the story of Ruth.

> ❷ *What would you say to someone who thinks they're not the right kind of person to be a Christian?*

> ❷ *What would you say to someone who is finding it hard to trust God's plans?*

> ❷ *What would you say to someone who feels far away from God's loving care?*

EASTER: Shadows

To explain his death and resurrection, Jesus continually pointed back to events from the past, recorded in the Old Testament. After he rose, his apostles did the same.

So to understand the message of Easter, and to appreciate the wonder of Easter, we can look back to God's work in human history. The gospel is written throughout the pages of the Old Testament, in the lives and experiences of dozens of men and women. This Easter, we are going to enjoy ten shadows of the first Easter.

Read Genesis 3:1-24

The setting is Eden: a perfect garden for God's people to live in, enjoying relationship with him. The only "no" God gives is eating the fruit of one tree, the tree of the knowledge of good and evil, which represents authority and rule (Genesis 2:16-17).

Promises

❷ *Why does the woman eat the fruit (Genesis 3:6)? Why does the man eat it?*

❷ *In response, what does God do (v 16-19, 23-24)?*

❷ *But what will God provide (v 15)?*

God keeps his promises; and so he keeps his promise of 2:16-17. Mankind is judged, and will die. The rest of human history can be described as our attempt to get back to Eden: to rediscover peace, push back death, and reclaim immortality. Genesis 3:24 shows this is futile; Eden is out of the reach of sinful man. But verse 15 promises this is possible; God has promised to do what we cannot: to provide a human who will crush

Satan's head, even as Satan bites his heel. This offspring of Eve's will reverse humanity's captivity to Satan, crushing him even as he himself is bitten.

Read Luke 11:14-22

❷ *And even as humanity is banished from Eden, what does God do for them (Genesis 3:21)?*

God covers their shame, and ensures their survival. But it takes a death to provide these clothes. It is another glimmer of the day when a man's flesh would be broken and his blood poured out to cover our shame, and ensure our eternal survival.

Excuses

❷ *When God confronted the first humans with their sin, how did they reply (v 12-13)?*

We are genetically predisposed to pass the spiritual buck, to excuse our sin, to blame another. And we will never understand Good Friday until we admit who we are, what we have done, and what we are like. It's only as we own our sin and confront our sinfulness that we are able to bring it to the cross and see the Lord taking it and covering it.

Pray

Do so now. Bring your sin to the cross.

Two sons, one mountain

God's promises to Abraham, and through him to the world—people, land, blessing— all rested on his son, Isaac. Then God asked him something almost incomprehensible.

Take your son

Read Genesis 22:1-19

- ❓ *What must Abraham do (v 2)? Where?*
- ❓ *Why does Isaac not die (v 11-14)?*
- ❓ *Read John 3:16. What similarities do you see between what Abraham was willing to do, and what God did do?*

God did not ask Abraham to do anything he himself would not do. Isaac was laid on a wooden altar; God's Son was laid on a wooden cross. But there was no stand-in for Jesus. He was the stand-in. God sacrificed his only Son, not out of obedience but out of love. And where did he do this? In Jerusalem, a city built on a mountain which centuries before had a different name: Mount Moriah. As Abraham prepared to give his beloved son, we see a shocking, moving shadow of how God would give his beloved Son. As we look in our mind's eye at that hill, and at the wooden cross on which the Son of God was sacrificed as our stand-in, we know: *The Lord did provide.*

We will come back

Abraham is a great example of the kind of trusting, radical obedience that God calls his people to live by. But it was not blind obedience.

- ❓ *What is strange about Abraham's use of the word "we" in Genesis 22:5?*

Read Hebrews 11:17-19

How did Abraham know that, somehow, God would keep his promise in impossible circumstances, perhaps even by raising the dead? Probably because he had seen God do this before. Isaac's life had begun in the impossible place of Abraham's wife Sarah's barren womb, when she was too old to have children. Yet God promised her a child— and he kept his promise. So Abraham learned that the Lord is "the God who gives life to the dead and calls into being things that were not" (Romans 4:17). As he clambered up Mount Moriah, Abraham seems to have trusted that what God had done once, he would do again. If needs be, he would raise his son from the dead.

Of course, God instead provided a stand-in. But again, we see a shadow of Easter. For there would come a day when God would raise a Son from the dead.

⌃ Pray

Look at Mount Moriah in your mind. See the son, carrying the wood up the hill. See him laid on the place of sacrifice. See that son die, by the father's authority. See the Father, giving up his beloved Son. And know he did it out of love for you. And then see the Son returning alive, and know that the Father raised his Son out of love for him.

Then praise the God who gave his Son for you, and who gave life to the dead.

God wins

Abraham's family multiplied, but they ended up as slaves in Egypt. God freed them, by providing a lamb (just as in Abraham's day), who died in place of their firstborn.

But as they walk out of Egypt, they face a terrifying foe—Pharaoh's army.

On the western shore

Read Exodus 14:5-29

> ❓ *How do the Israelites respond as the Egyptians bear down on them (v 10)?*
> ❓ *What do they say to Moses (v 11-12)?*

Verses 11-12 show that the people's cry "to the LORD" (v 10) is one of panic, not faith.

> ❓ *What does Moses tell the people (v 14)? What does he promise God will do?*
> ❓ *How does God fight for his people and win (v 15-18, 21-29)?*

The people learned on the two shores of the Red Sea: *Don't be frightened—God wins.* He rescued his people by crushing his enemies through the work of his servant, the leader of his people.

We face a far worse enemy than Satan—implacable, invincible death.

> ❓ *Read Romans 6:8-9. How did God fight death for his people, and win?*

On the eastern shore

Read Exodus 14:30 – 15:6

> ❓ *How do the people respond in:*
> • *14:31 (and how is this different to their response in v 10-12)?*
> • *15:1-6?*

How do we respond to the death of death? Just as the Israelites responded to the death of Pharaoh's army. With awed respect for God, with total trust in his rescuing servant, Jesus, and with a song of joyful praise, celebrating his victory.

🔽 Apply

> ❓ *Are there times when you feel as the Israelites did in Exodus 14:10-12, wishing you could just live like the rest of the world?*
> ❓ *This Easter, how will meditating on the truth that your death died when your King died encourage you to travel through the wilderness towards his presence, instead of turning back to slavery to sin?*

🔼 Pray

Your death may seem a long way off, or very close. The events of Easter enable you to sing this song as you consider your death: no longer is it a defeat, but rather, a doorway into the presence of your conquering Lord.

Thine be the glory, risen, conquering Son;
endless is the victory, thou o'er death hast won;
angels in bright raiment rolled the stone away,
kept the folded grave clothes where thy body lay.
Thine be the glory, risen, conquering Son,
Endless is the victory, thou o'er death hast won.

Sing this song now as a prayer of praise to him.

Snakes on a plain

With Egypt behind them, God's people travelled to God's land. But one of their worst enemies went with them—themselves.

Problem

Read Numbers 21:4-9

❓ *What do the people complain about?*

The "miserable food" is the manna God had miraculously provided (Exodus 16). The people are effectively saying: *We don't want to live with and rely on you in this world.* In sending the poisonous snakes, God says, *Ok, you won't.* Poisonous snakes were normal in the desert; miraculous food was not. The people have chosen life without God and his protection and blessing, a life complete with suffering and death.

···· TIME OUT ·····································

Read Romans 1:18-32

❓ *What is being revealed (v 18)?*

❓ *Why (v 18, 21, 28)?*

And this judgment is seen in God giving us what we want. We choose a life without him; he allows us to have it, just as in the desert with Israel. He gives people who reject life with him what they want, all the way into hell.

Solution

❓ *Who provides the solution, and how (Numbers 21:8-9)?*

❓ *What did an Israelite bitten by a snake and facing death need to do (v 9)?*

Read John 3:14-15

❓ *What does Jesus say God was pointing to in this wilderness incident?*

In his judgment, God gives us what we choose; but in his mercy, he offers us what we need. He rescues people from the consequences of their own decisions. He did it through a bronze snake when his people were facing certain death; he has, supremely, done it eternally through the Lord Jesus when we were facing certain hell. And as a stricken Israelite needed only to look at the bronze snake lifted up on a pole in order to be healed, we need only to look with the eyes of faith at the bloodied body of Christ lifted up on his cross in order to be saved.

☑ Apply

The English preacher Charles Simeon once said it was only as he understood the depths of his own sin that he could appreciate the greatness of the cross of Jesus.

❓ *Do you see yourself as bitten by the venom of judgment, facing hell because you chose to sin? Or as quite a nice person, just with a few flaws?*

❓ *Do you truly see Jesus, lifted up, as the only way you can avoid the consequences of your own choice to rebel?*

Speak to Jesus now. Use Numbers 21:7 and 9 to confess your sin and look to Jesus.

Not just a rescuer

God brought his people into the land he'd promised under Joshua, Moses' successor. But their hearts had not changed, and they continued to fail to obey God.

So God allowed their enemies to defeat and oppress them, just as he had allowed the snakes in the desert to bite them. But, true to his character, he also provided a rescue, in the form of "judges", whom he raised up to lead his people and defeat their enemies. One of these was Deborah...

A true leader

Read Judges 4:1-15

> ❷ *When the previous judge, Ehud, died, what then happened to Israel?*
>
> • *v 1*
> • *v 2*
>
> ❷ *When the people cry for help, who are we introduced to, and what is she doing (v 4-5)?*

In Judges, each judge's main role is usually to fight and defeat Israel's enemies.

> ❷ *What is different about Deborah (v 6-7)?*

Of all the judges, Deborah comes closest to being a godly ruler, rather than only a rescuer. Among the warrior-leaders of the book of Judges, Deborah reminds us that God's people need a ruler to lead them in obedience, not just a rescuer to lead them out of oppression. The perfect judge would do both...

... and the perfect judge would never die, because (as we saw in verse 1) peace was never permanent since the leaders were always temporary. Death always got in the way.

An amazing leader

Read Matthew 7:24-29

> ❷ *What was the difference between the leadership of the teachers of the law and the leadership of Jesus (v 29)?*
>
> ❷ *What is the right thing to do with Jesus' words of authority (v 24-25)?*

Jesus did come to rescue God's people (whereas Deborah did not); but he also came to rule them (as Deborah did). Good Friday would not be "good" if it were not followed by Easter Sunday. The cross opens the way into the kingdom; the empty tomb establishes who the King of the kingdom is, and proclaims that this kingdom will never end, for its King shall never die. Without Jesus' death, we could not live in the kingdom; without Jesus' resurrection, there would be no kingdom. **Read Revelation 1:9-18.**

🔼 Pray

Use Revelation 1:18 to praise Jesus that his death is behind him, and so will never be ahead of him. Praise him for his authority over death and Hades.

Ask Jesus to give you not only a greater appreciation of his rescue this Easter week, but a renewed appreciation of and obedience to his rule.

Bible in a year: Deuteronomy 14 – 17

Arms outstretched

Because each judge dies, the people keep forgetting God and disobeying him, and so falling prey to their enemies. And each time, the sin and the oppression are worse.

Birth

Read Judges 13:1-5, 24-25

This time, the Philistines are the oppressors.

> ❷ *How does God take the initiative to begin to save his people (v 3)?*
>
> ❷ *What is remarkable about this pregnancy (v 2-3)?*
>
> ❷ *What role will this child have (v 5)?*

Samson is blessed by the Lord and stirred by his Spirit (v 24-25), but then things go off-track. Far from fighting the Philistines, he falls in love with one of them (14:1-2); he fails to keep to his Nazirite vow (he touches a dead animal, v 8-9); he only uses his Spirit-given strength in anger or self-defence (v 19; 15:3-5, 7-8, 14-15); and he ends up living with a Philistine, Delilah, who betrays him into the hands of his enemies (16:5-6). He becomes a weak, blind captive (v 21-22).

Death

Read Judges 16:23-31

> ❷ *How does Samson end up (v 30)?*
>
> ❷ *What does he achieve (v 30)?*

Between the angelic announcement of his birth and the victorious defeat of his death, there was not much good in Samson's life. But in his death, we see so many echoes of another man who would die in weakness and in triumph.

- Both Samson and he were betrayed by people close to them.
- Both Samson and he were handed over to Gentile oppressors.
- Both Samson and he were tortured and put on display for public mockery.
- Both Samson and he died with their arms outstretched and a prayer on their lips.
- Both Samson and he looked utterly defeated, and yet were achieving the greatest victory of their lives.

Both Samson and he achieved in their deaths what an angel announced to their parents would be the purpose of their lives: Samson would "take the lead in delivering Israel from the hands of the Philistines" (13:5); he would be given "the name Jesus, because he will save his people from their sins" (Matthew 1:21).

Yet while Samson was in the temple of Dagon because of his own weaknesses and disobedience, Jesus was in the clutches of death because of ours. And whereas Samson's story finishes with his burial and the end of his rule (Judges 16:30-31), Jesus' burial was just the beginning of the story, and the prelude to his rule.

🔼 Pray

Here is your greater Samson, your Rescuer. Praise him now for all he did for you. And praise him that his death was not his end.

Bible in a year: Deuteronomy 18 • John 5 • Acts 3

Slaying the snake

In Genesis 3:15, God promised to send a man who would defeat the serpent, Satan, at the very moment when the "snake" seemed strongest. But centuries passed…

It is now 1100 BC, and Israel has a king, Saul. Saul is the king the people want, but he is not the king they need. So, even as Saul sits on the throne, God has rejected him and anointed a new king, a king-in-waiting: the shepherd-boy David.

Read 1 Samuel 17:1-24

❷ *Where are the Philistines (v 1)?*

This is the heartland of Israel.

❷ *What is Goliath's challenge (v 8-10)?*

Read 1 Samuel 17:25-54

❷ *How do Saul and David react differently to Goliath (v 11, 32, 37)?*

Israel may have forgotten God; David has not!

In describing Goliath, "coat of scale armour" (v 5) is literally "coat of scales". Here is an enemy of God's people, terrorising and dominating them, covered in scales. Goliath is like a snake—an invincible one.

❷ *What does God's chosen king do (v 48-49)?*

❷ *How does he do this, and how doesn't he do this (v 50—see also v 38-40)?*

God has defeated the great snake through his chosen king, and at the moment when the snake seems strongest. Goliath was sure he had won (v 42-44); in fact, he was about to be crushed. And God's chosen king did not use the weapons of this world, or have

the appearance of the kings of this world. But he would win the victory for his people.

Read John 12:27-33

Here is God's ultimate chosen King, the Lord Jesus, the greater descendant of King David (see God's promise to David in 2 Samuel 7:12-16). At the moment when Satan, the "prince of this world", seemed to have utterly defeated Christ by killing him, he was, in fact, crushed. God's chosen King did not use the weapons of this world to render Satan powerless; he used his own blood. He did not have the appearance of a great king as he hung on the cross, bleeding and dying; but he was winning victory for his people.

▾ Apply

Re-read 1 Samuel 17:11 and 51-53

❷ *What difference to the Israelites' confidence did David's victory make?*

We don't fight Philistines. But we do battle our sin, and we do struggle to tell others the gospel. But we can know victory in both, just as Israel did as they pursued the Philistines and plundered their camp; because the victory is already won.

❷ *What difference to your confidence in fighting sin and sharing your faith will Jesus' victory make to you today?*

Washed clean

After David and his son Solomon, the kings and the people did not seek to obey God; and their enemies, including Aram, began to invade and dominate them once more.

Read 2 Kings 5:1-19

❷ *In what ways is Naaman both powerful and successful (v 1)?*

❷ *What is his only problem (v 1)?*

Not only was this a painful, incurable disease that often led to death; it was a sign of spiritual uncleanness that always led to exclusion from God's presence (see Numbers 5:1-3).

❷ *How does Naaman hear about God's prophet, and from whom (2 Kings 5:2-5)?*

❷ *Why do you think he takes a vast weight of silver and gold with him?*

Elisha sends his messenger out to speak to Naaman and tell him how he can be healed (v 10).

❷ *So why does Naaman very nearly end up not healed (v 10-13)?*

It seems from verses 11 and 14 that Naaman expected either a show of great power from Elisha, or to be given a great challenge for him to achieve and then be given healing. And all the wealth he brought suggests that Naaman assumed he would need to offer something in the first place. But all Elisha says is: *Wash in the Jordan River seven times and you will be healed.* That was neither powerful, nor challenging. But it was utterly effective (v 14). And it was completely free—Elisha "will not accept a thing" (v 16) except Naaman's confession that "there is no God in all the world except in Israel" (v 15).

Many people's problem with the gospel is that its simplicity completely strips away our pride. God says, *Trust a man dying on a cross, and you will be saved.* And we think, *Is that it? Surely I have to offer something? Surely I must do something? Surely being saved looks more impressive than that?* It is hard to believe that God has done everything; it is hard to trust in such a surprising method of salvation. Peter had the same problem as Naaman; **read John 13:3-9.**

⌄ Apply

❷ *Do you ever find yourself believing that you must earn God's ongoing salvation; or that you must pay him back for your salvation?*

Naaman heard about God's prophet from his slave, who was risking her life by speaking, and had every reason to dislike Naaman and keep quiet.

❷ *How does her willingness to speak encourage and challenge you this Easter?*

❷ *Who is the Spirit prompting you to tell: "There is a Saviour, who can cure you of your sin-sickness?"*

⌃ Pray

Use John 13:8-9 to admit your need of Jesus' work, and thank him for it.

Into the depths

Jonah was a prophet who was happy to prophesy blessing for his own people (2 Kings 14:23-25), but very unhappy about the possibility of his enemies being blessed.

So unhappy that he tried to run from God...

Jonah

Rather than warn the Ninevites of God's judgment and give them time to repent, Jonah sailed in the opposite direction. God sent a storm to stop Jonah, and Jonah told the sailors to throw him overboard, since the storm was his fault.

Read Jonah 1:15 – 3:5, 10

❓ How does Jonah describe the experience of sinking down in the water (2:2, 6)?

❓ Why doesn't he die (1:17, 2:10)?

❓ When Jonah obeys God at the second opportunity and warns the Ninevites, how do they respond (3:5)?

❓ And how does God respond to them (v 10)?

And all this should point us to Jesus. We know this because Jesus said so...

One greater than Jonah

Read Matthew 12:22-24, 38-41

When Jesus heals a demon-possessed, blind man, the Pharisees decide that this sign of his identity is actually due to satanic power (v 24); and then they demand from him—a sign (v 38)!

❓ What does Jesus say is the only sign they'll get (v 39)?

❓ How does he explain what he means, in verse 40?

People in our day, just as back then, demand more proof—more signs—that he really is the Son of God, that what he says about judgment and salvation really is true. And most Christians experience sudden moments or prolonged periods of doubt: *Is it really true? How can I be sure?* Jesus says, *I have already given you the clearest sign you could ever have—my death, burial and resurrection. The Ninevites knew Jonah was a prophet of God and they needed to listen to him because he had gone down into the depths, had been effectively dead for three days, and then had come back to the land of the living. You can know that I am the Son of God and you need to listen to me because I went down into the depths, I was literally dead for three days, and then I came back to life.*

❓ What is the only sensible response, as the Ninevites show us (v 41)?

☑ Apply

This Easter, be in no doubt that Jesus is the Son of God, and now submit to him as your King. The Easter events are the clearest sign the world will ever have, and the only sign the world should need. When you doubt, look to the historical events of the first Easter. And as you do that, be a Ninevite—repent of your sin and enjoy God's compassion.

The forgiving husband

Thirty years after Jonah, there was another prophet in Israel. And his personal life gives us a startling glimpse of who we are, and what God has done for us in Jesus.

An adulterous wife

Read Hosea 1:2-9

❓ *What does God tell Hosea to do (v 2)? What is this marriage a picture of (v 2)?*

❓ *What do her children's names warn Israel will happen to them (v 4, 6, 8-9)?*

Spiritual adultery. That is what Israel was guilty of, by loving other things instead of the God who had loved them, committed himself to them, given them a home, provided for them, and been their perfect, divine Husband. They had turned their backs on a marriage literally made in heaven in order to prostitute themselves with idols.

Spiritual adultery. That is what we are guilty of, whenever we choose to love and trust anything other than the God who has done so much for us. We may belittle sin to ourselves and excuse it in each other, but God calls us what we are: spiritual adulterers who do not deserve his love or blessing.

🔼 Pray

The question is not whether we are guilty, but whether we will accept this truth. Spend some time now being real with God about your own unfaithfulness.

A loving husband

Read Hosea 3:1-6

❓ *What does God tell Hosea to do (v 1)?*

Gomer has left her husband, and appears to be living as the lover and possession of another man. Her adultery has left her trapped—she is a slave, who must be bought back, or redeemed (v 2).

❓ *What is remarkable about Hosea's actions in verse 2?*

Verse 3 is a declaration of a complete restoration of relationship. It is, in a sense, a resurrection—new life. Gomer had sold herself into slavery; Hosea has bought her back so that she can enjoy married life again, living as his wife. He has paid the price she never could so that she can know again the relationship she had given up.

Read 1 Peter 1:18-19

❓ *What was the cost of our redemption?*

When the New Testament describes the church as Jesus' bride, it is describing us as Gomer: as adulterers, bought back by our Husband at the cost of his own blood, so that we can know the joy of living with him, the one we were made for. This is why we live to please the risen, reigning Jesus: because we know what he bought us out of, and we know what it cost; and so we love the one who loves us so much, and so undeservedly.

🔼 Pray

Let the picture of Hosea buying Gomer back to live as his wife move you to thank your Husband right now.

HE GIVES MORE GRACE

30 Hope-Filled Reflections for the
Ups and Downs of Motherhood

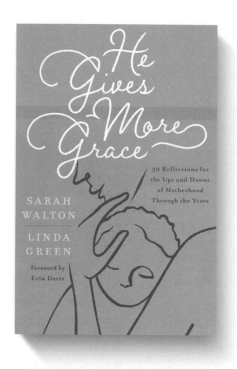

Daily encouragement from God's word for
mothers with children of all ages. Feel less
pressure and more joy as you focus on the
work of Jesus rather than your own efforts.

MARK FOR YOU

Expository Guide to

Mark's Gospel

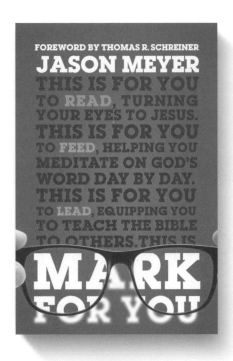

This accessible, absorbing guide is more applied than
a typical commentary, making it a great resource for
personal devotion, as well as useful for leading small-
group studies or for sermon preparation.

thegoodbook.co.uk/mark-for-you
thegoodbook.com/mark-for-you

Introduce a friend to

explore

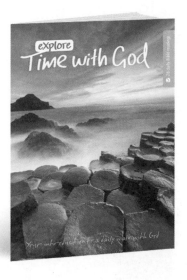

If you're enjoying using *Explore*, why not introduce a friend? Time with God is our introduction to daily Bible reading and is a great way to get started with a regular time with God. It includes 28 daily readings along with articles, advice and practical tips on how to apply what the passage teaches.

Why not order a copy for someone you would like to encourage?

Coming up next…

- **Mark**
  with Jason Meyer and Catherine Durant

- **1 Thessalonians**
  with Ligon Duncan

- **Ezekiel**
  with Garrett Conner

- **Philippians**
  with Steven Lawson and Carl Laferton

 Don't miss your copy. Contact your local Christian bookshop or church agent, or visit:

UK & Europe: thegoodbook.co.uk
info@thegoodbook.co.uk
Tel: 0333 123 0880

North America: thegoodbook.com
info@thegoodbook.com
Tel: 866 244 2165

Australia & New Zealand:
thegoodbook.com.au
info@thegoodbook.com.au
Tel: (02) 9564 3555

South Africa: www.christianbooks.co.za
orders@christianbooks.co.za
Tel: 021 674 6931/2